The
LIGHT
That Was
Dark

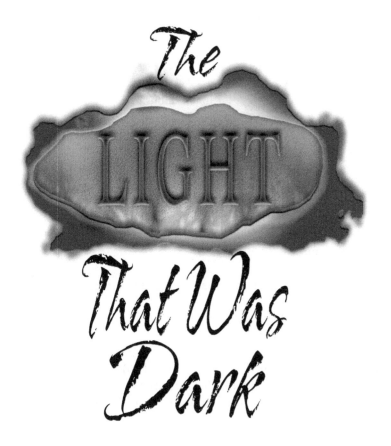

The LIGHT That Was Dark

From the New Age

to Amazing Grace

WARREN SMITH

MOUNTAIN STREAM PRESS

The Light That Was Dark
©1992, 2005 Warren Smith
Fifth Printing 2022
Mountain Stream Press

First Edition: August 1992, Northfield Publishing

The subtitle has been changed in this edition from "A Spiritual Journey" to "From the New Age to Amazing Grace," and except for some minor editing and a new Prologue and Epilogue, the original 1992 text remains the same.

Some names of individuals have been changed to protect their privacy.

All Scripture quotations, unless otherwise indicated, are taken from the Authorized King James Bible.

**To order additional copies of this book, call 866-876-3910.
For international orders, call 541-391-7699.**

Publisher's Cataloging-in-Publication Data
Smith, Warren, 1945-
The light that was dark: from the new age to amazing grace / Warren Smith—2nd ed.
1. Christianity 2. New Age Spirituality 3. The New Spirituality
Library of Congress Control Number: 2008921635
ISBN 0-9763492-1-3
(previously published by Northfield Publishing, an imprint of Moody Press, ISBN 1-881273-06-7)

Printed in the United States of America.

To Joy,

my partner, my help meet,
my wife, and my friend,
for your spiritual discernment,
your insistence on truth,
your long-suffering love,
and your faith in God

Acknowledgments

I would like to thank all the people who supported me in the initial writing and publication of this book. I would also like to thank everyone who helped me to bring this book back into print. Most of all, I would like to thank God for shining His light into the darkness and showing us the way.

Contents

Prologue

One bright winter's day many years ago, I cross-country skied along the well-marked Dewey Point Trail in Yosemite National Park. Shooting in and out of the pine trees on the newly fallen Sierra snow, I made my way toward trail's end. When I reached the Dewey Point lookout, I was several thousand feet above the valley floor. Yosemite Valley stretched out spectacularly before me in the distance. Fellow skiers who had already arrived were sitting on the rocks eating and drinking and taking in the wondrous scenery.

I sat down next to a man who was intently studying a topographic map of the area. We immediately entered into conversation. He was a city planner from northern California. He told me that rather than taking the main trail back to the Badger Pass Trailhead, he was considering an alternative cross-country journey that would take him off the established trail. He showed me his contemplated route. I wasn't particularly skilled at reading topographic maps, but his alternative plan seemed simple and straightforward. Buoyed by the beauty of my surroundings and intrigued by his proposed journey, I asked if I could join him. He seemed so confident and authoritative that I was sure he had the wherewithal to safely guide us to our destination.

An hour or so later, we departed from the Dewey Point Trail and skied off into the woods. The sky was deep blue above us, and the freshly fallen snow made for great skiing. What an adventure! It was exhilarating as we skied through Yosemite's back country heading for Badger Pass. I followed my new friend's lead. Occasionally, as we stopped to rest he would glance at his map. I was glad that he knew what he was doing.

Several hours into our trek, I sensed something was wrong. My friend looked perplexed as he consulted his map. He said that we should have reached our destination by now. Maybe Badger Pass was just up ahead. But it wasn't. We stopped again. Now he was really concerned. My heart sank when he said that he had lost his bearings and we might actually be heading into a treacherous wilderness area. Neither of us had sleeping bags or adequate provisions. The euphoria we had been feeling disappeared altogether when we realized that we could both die out there in the snow.

By late afternoon, I was in a state of near panic. Although not a particularly spiritual or religious person, I found myself muttering, "Help me God, help me God" over and over again as we skied through the woods. A tangible sense of fear gripped my entire being as the evening started to settle in. How could this happen? My new friend and guide had seemed so knowledgeable and sure of himself. It had never occurred to me that we might get lost. What had been a wonderful and exciting adventure was now a living nightmare.

With night almost completely upon us, we saw what looked to be a faded trail marker. My friend checked his map once again. We were ecstatic as we were finally able to pinpoint our general location. It seemed that we had stumbled upon a rarely used trail which would lead us directly to our destination. Overjoyed at finding this old trail, we followed the faded markers in the moonlight for another hour or so. Grateful, but thoroughly exhausted, we finally reached the parking lot. We could hardly believe our good fortune.

As we talked and laughed and sighed a great sigh of relief, I was determined never to put myself in that kind of situation again. But one of the lessons I thought I had learned that day—putting unwarranted trust in people who seem more knowledgeable than myself—was one that I would have to learn all over again when I started exploring the spiritual realm. *The Light That Was Dark* is my take on Amazing Grace—how I once was lost but now am found.

**Take heed therefore that the light
which is in thee be not darkness.**
Luke 11:35

One

Seeing the Psychic

I sat quietly in the nicely decorated living room of the apartment where Bonnie was doing psychic readings. I had ten minutes until my appointment, and I shifted anxiously in my chair. Although much of my resistance to psychics and psychic things had decreased since meeting Kay, I was still uneasy.

My recent interest in the friendly, dark-haired waitress at a popular downtown restaurant had resulted in my asking her to come to my house one evening. In the course of our evening's conversation, I found that she liked the music of John Prine and had at least a passing interest in metaphysics. The next day I bought two John Prine albums, and now here I was seeing a friend of a friend of hers who was a visiting psychic.

As I waited for my reading, I remembered the reassurance I had felt when Kay first told me about Bonnie. I wondered why I had resisted psychic things in the past. It was probably my conservative East Coast upbringing. Whatever the case, I'd always had the impression that people who were involved in metaphysics and the occult were eccentric and far-out. But the ease with which Kay talked about metaphysical matters helped me overcome my prejudice. Thanks to her, it now seemed acceptable and practical and down-to-earth.

Although Kay had legitimized an area I had always considered taboo, I was still nervous about how the reading would work. The idea of being psychically and spiritually examined made me uncomfortable. I wasn't sure what Bonnie would find. I knew I wasn't the most together person in the world. Thirty-three years old and I still hadn't found whatever it was I was looking for.

My job as a social worker was mildly satisfying but not deeply fulfilling, and the relationships I had with the people in my life continued to be largely superficial and illusive. It was all too clear that my years of introspection had produced only fragments of what I considered to be real personal growth. I was tired of traditional and pop psychology, but more than anything I had grown weary of my own tedious self-examination. I was definitely ready for something new. I wanted a change, but I knew that change meant risk and taking risks was never easy. As frightened as I was, though, about the uncertainties of the reading, my desire for change was greater than my fear of psychic exposure. Maybe it would push me in the right direction. Maybe Bonnie could help me.

2

Suddenly it was time. The friend of Kay's, whose apartment Bonnie was using, ushered me into the back room. Bonnie smiled as we were introduced, and I thought, *Welcome to the world of psychic readings!* For a moment I felt as if I had stepped onto a huge metaphysical stage. I felt vulnerable and self-conscious as I strained to maintain eye contact with Bonnie. Even her unpretentious appearance and gentle, friendly manner could not put me at ease. I was convinced that I was about to get the spiritual equivalent of an Army physical. I wondered if she was already checking out my aura.

She had to be picking up on my nervousness, and I suspected that she was trying to make me feel more comfortable when she started talking about her background as a psychic reader. She told me that she had been intuitive as a young girl but that it had taken considerable discipline and study to get to the point of actually doing readings.

Bonnie was about my age. She had short blonde hair and a simple unaffected appearance. She was confident and relaxed. When she saw that I was more at ease, she put the cassette tape I had been told to bring into her tape recorder, pushed the record button, and the session was on.

I immediately lost whatever composure I had gained. I could feel my heart pounding as we sat in silence for what seemed an eternity, though it was probably only a minute or so. She was starting to zero in on me, and I couldn't help but wonder what she was seeing. I tried to relax, but it was no use.

"I am having trouble finding your aura," she said at last. She sounded perplexed and surprised, as if that was unusual, even strange. My worst fears rose to the surface. It seemed bizarre to sit there as she hunted for my missing aura.

This is *awful*, I thought. *I don't even have an aura.* I had been prepared for a bad reading but not for no reading at all. I felt embarrassed and ashamed.

"Your aura is very black," was her next bit of news, and it hurt. I struggled to keep calm, but I felt smashed inside. I wanted to get up and leave.

When I thought that I could not sit there another moment she spoke again. "I am now starting to see a little more."

She appeared to be relieved, and so was I, of course. Knowing that I actually had an aura at this point was almost grounds for celebration.

But before I had a chance to get too carried away, she said that from what she *could* see I was spiritually underdeveloped. Not at all what I wanted to hear.

She said that I had overemphasized the physical and mental aspects of my life and that they were highly disproportionate to the spiritual part of my being. It looked as if I had almost completely ignored my spiritual life.

She was right. I *had* ignored spiritual things most of my life. I had always been active in sports and had stayed away from anything spiritual. Most of my reading had been in the areas of psychology and self-help, maybe an occasional book by a Zen poet, but that was

about it in the mystical realm. My attempts to better myself had
been no-nonsense and concrete.

Bonnie said that I needed to open myself up to spiritual things,
to begin developing my spiritual self, to stop using my head so
much, and to open my heart. I definitely needed to become more
balanced. Her comments were sincere, and I felt no judgment from
her, although I was still feeling a little put down by the way things
had gone so far. But I was starting to get the idea that it was nothing
personal. She was just telling me what she saw, and she wasn't pull-
ing any punches. The honesty was disarming.

Proceeding to distinguish what she could from my aura, Bonnie
went on to describe character traits and personality quirks that only
someone close to me would know. She was amazingly accurate in
discussing some of my most recent relationships and was also surprisingly on target in describing specific situations I was dealing
with at work. Her abilities as a psychic were clearly evident.

It was toward the end of the reading that I first noticed the
whirling sensation over my head. I tried to ignore it, but it wouldn't
go away. It was a strange but not unpleasant feeling that seemed to
flutter and vibrate and even tingle above me. I was startled when
Bonnie picked up on it.

"Are you aware that there is a ball of light over your head?"

I was dumbfounded. A ball of light? Is that what I was feeling?
This was getting a little wild.

I told Bonnie that I had been feeling *something* over my head
but didn't know what it was. She said it again.

"It's a ball of light."

For a moment I tried to understand what a ball of light was
doing over my head. Then I asked the obvious.

"Why is there a ball of light over my head?"

"You are being shown that you have a lot of help on the other
side," she said matter-of-factly.

"What do you mean by 'the other side'?"

"The spirit world," was her quick reply. "Family and loved ones who have passed away, as well as angels and other spirits who for whatever reasons are sympathetic to your life. They are making themselves known to you. They are reaching out to you and letting you know that they are available if you want their help." Bonnie was smiling; she seemed pleased by this show of support.

I was intrigued that there was a spirit world and flattered by its interest in me. I asked Bonnie to elaborate.

"Those on the other side know what you are going through. Although they are making themselves known to you, they will not involve themselves in your life without your permission. If you want their help you will have to ask."

"Ask?" I was getting confused.

"Yes. Just ask. It's a permission within your being that can be expressed inwardly or outwardly. They will know if you want their help." Bonnie seemed so knowledgeable that I trusted what she said.

We were both encouraged by the turn of events. The reading had been difficult for both of us up to that point. But then out of nowhere had come this supernatural ball of light, this offer of support.

I sat back in my chair trying to comprehend it. *How amazing,* I thought, *that we can reach out to the spirit world. A spiritual dimension is really out there, willing and able to help us.* I knew in that moment that I wanted its help. I understood that the ball of light had come at a perfect time in the reading and in my life. It had given me a much needed sense of validation. I felt better about myself knowing that somewhere out there in the universe I was really cared for. Suddenly I didn't feel alone. As far as I was concerned, the ball of light had been an act of compassion, and I was grateful.

At the end of the reading I paid Bonnie and left feeling upbeat. I had a new confidence and resolve about my spiritual life. The next step was up to me.

3

Later that afternoon back at my little canyon home, I went out to the creek and thought about the reading. I knew I needed help in my spiritual life. Over the years I had neglected it badly with all my concerns about *this* world. For some reason church never clicked for me as a kid. And later affiliations with church groups had always left me feeling empty. Once I got to college I forgot about church altogether.

But today was different. Though the reading had been a definite spiritual experience, it had nothing to do with church. I liked Bonnie's intuitive, straightforward, and confrontational brand of spirituality, with its emphasis on personal and spiritual growth. It was much different from the spirituality of my youth. This was no Sunday-as-usual religion. Metaphysical spirituality was relevant, tangible, and real. And I could feel this new spirituality reaching out to me through Kay and Bonnie and the ball of light. I almost felt as if I was being called, and I wanted to respond.

After dinner, I got my sleeping bag out of the closet and climbed up on top of my flat-roofed house. It was a clear evening. I spread my bag out onto the middle of the roof and lay there peacefully and contentedly as night settled in on the canyon. Lying on my back, I looked straight up into the night sky. I watched the stars come out one by one, getting clearer and clearer as they dotted the heavens in all directions. It was a special night, and I was filled with anticipation and excitement. Somehow I understood that tonight would serve as a new beginning for me. I was about to take off on an amazing spiritual journey. But I also knew that before I did, I needed to reflect on my life thus far. I wanted to be able to remember and appreciate my past as it had brought me to this present moment.

As I stared into the sky, I remembered my hometown of Westport, Connecticut. I thought of my dad stepping off the commuter train from New York and helping to coach my Little League baseball team. The thrill of excitement when I hit a home run. The bitter disappointment when I struck out and let the team down.

I remembered the inevitable disagreements that happen in a family, as well as the games of Parcheesi®, the nights of watching Jackie Gleason, the Sunday breakfasts on the Long Island Sound, and my checking Mickey Mantle's batting average in the *New York Times*. I recalled my dad's special poems at Christmas, my mom's strawberry pancakes, skating with my girlfriend on Nash's Pond, and how my parents had always been there no matter what.

I knew that I had not been very happy as a child. God knows my parents had done their best. But perhaps something within me was not at peace even then.

My way of running away from home was to volunteer for boarding school at age fifteen—The Hill School in Pottstown, Pennsylvania. I could still hear the bell ringing, see four hundred and fifty people sitting down to eat at the same time, and see the cherry bombs we used to set off in front of the study hall with their fuses in the unlighted ends of Pall Mall cigarettes—all of us back in our rooms studying when the cigarettes finally burned down and the explosions went off. And I will never forget my surprise at being elected captain of the school's baseball team.

Then on to the University of Pennsylvania—those aimless, purposeless days of rebellion and ramming around, the 2:00 A.M. skateboarding on city streets, my singing on stage with the band at the Philly Mixer, the crazy parties, the punched out windows and all the people down at Carney's Bar. Surviving a difficult senior year when drinking no longer got me high, I graduated by the skin of my teeth, not having the slightest idea of what I would do with my life.

I remembered not having to decide because the Army decided for me—somehow getting an assignment at the White House rather than a foxhole in Viet Nam, meeting President and Lady Bird Johnson, going into the National League dugout with my friend at the 1969 All Star game at RFK Stadium with our White House badges and pretending to be Secret Service agents, and spending the whole game in the dugout with our childhood heroes.

Still in the Army but retreating further and further inside myself, I read *Man's Search for Himself, Who Am I?*, and every other psychological, self-seeking book I could lay my hands on, as I holed up in my room listening to songs such as Neil Young's "The Loner." I recalled being so cut-off, confused, and depressed that I finally saw a therapist, pouring out my soul in that first session but then going nowhere in the next four or five, his impersonal Freudian manner, my interest waning.

I remembered getting out of the Army, going back home, ending up driving a cab out of the Westport Railroad Station day after day, feeling alienated from my friends and family, needing to leave Westport and find myself, setting off one morning for San Francisco, looking back one last time at my mom and dad who were waving from the porch steps, driving west, spending that first night in a parking lot in Pittsburgh, unable to unlock the steering wheel the next morning and feeling overwhelmed and trapped, sleeping in a corn field in Iowa and on a picnic table in South Dakota, picking up a young hitchhiker in Reno who knew about a "crash pad" in San Francisco run by some "Jesus freaks," driving across the Golden Gate Bridge, the adrenaline rush as I saw San Francisco for the first time—it seemed so clean and white, spread out along the bay—the feeling of finally being home in that remarkable city.

That first night in the crash pad with all the lonely, lost, and strung-out people, I never guessed that they would become a major focus in my life for the next twenty years.

I recalled how I rode cable cars, explored the redwoods, cleaned carpets, did janitorial work, sold *Time-Life* nature books over the telephone, backpacked in Yosemite, loaded trucks at a nursery in Half-Moon Bay, walked the beaches, and ate hot fudge sundaes in Ghirardelli Square—and finally got a job as an eligibility worker at the San Francisco Department of Social Services. I liked the job so much that I took off to Tulane Graduate School to become a social worker.

New Orleans—that sad, wonderful, jazzy blues town on the Mississippi—where I studied while working as a resident counselor in a psychiatric halfway house a few blocks from school. Living on the same floor as my clients was wild—Johnny with his face half-blown away by a self-inflicted shotgun wound, pretty Sammy with his mirrored, high-heeled platform shoes and boyfriends in the Quarter, Henry and Tobias, both of whom would be dead by their own hands in less than two years.

My weekend escape away from the halfway house was a little studio in the French Quarter, and my landlady was a famous stripper on Bourbon Street. I would walk around the Quarter at night, smelling the fresh seafood, catching the sounds of laughter from the bars and listening to the old musicians playing their wonderful jazz at Preservation Hall.

And then there was the rainy Saturday morning and the jazz funeral I chanced upon across town. My grief over the death of someone I didn't even know overwhelmed me as I heard about a real Jesus in the hymns of the mourners—it was a hint of something spiritual that I could feel but didn't understand—"when the saints go marching in," death, eternity, mystery.

I graduated with an MSW and moved back to San Francisco. My relationship with Anne, once a stewardess but now a Cal Berkeley law student, came to an end. She had been my trusted, valued friend, but we were not to be, and eventually I met Kari.

I took a job as night social worker for Traveler's Aid at the Greyhound Bus Station in the San Francisco Tenderloin, working with stranded, destitute, and homeless people. I had no time to think about my own problems because I was so busy with everyone else's—the suicidal transvestite who had hung a noose from the light fixture in his Turk Street hotel room, the burned-out, beat-up hooker dumped off at the Greyhound by her pimp when she was all used up, the seventy-three-year-old man who had given up on life and was sitting in the Greyhound lobby waiting to die.

Counseling person after person, night after night, on the streets of San Francisco and in the Greyhound lobby, I met people who had fled to this city by the bay to start their lives again, just as I had. I supposedly helped them, but it was really they who had helped me. The job had been a gift.

I eventually decided to leave the city and move to the country. I remembered the drive to my new home in northern California, U-Haul in tow, and the trailer mysteriously unhooking from my pickup truck near Vallejo and actually passing me on the highway.

Then I worked as a psychiatric social worker with developmentally disabled people in residential care homes in our county. I remembered their simple love and acceptance—and my love and affection for them. After buying my little canyon home, I lived life the best I could, yet I still felt empty and alone.

Then earlier today came the reading from Bonnie. I lay there under the starry sky with this kaleidoscopic collage of images streaming through my mind. It had been a long, mysterious, exciting, yet unknown journey. Where was it heading?

Then suddenly I knew it was time. I took a deep breath and prayed out loud: "All you on the other side, I want your help in my life. I want to become more spiritual, I want to grow."

In the stillness, I could feel the importance of what I had just done. Taking one long, last look at the heavens, I curled up comfortably in my sleeping bag and went to sleep.

Two

Enter Rajneesh

I knew that something significant had been set in motion by my rooftop prayer. What I didn't know was that it would be a number of months before I received an obvious discernable answer. In the meantime, I found myself involved in a gradual ever-intensifying process that was preparing me for what was yet to come.

I told only a few close friends about my reading with Bonnie. Most of the people I knew would be skeptical, even critical, of a psychic reading—especially one that included an appearance by a ball of light. But I knew it was real. I had felt it, and Bonnie had seen it.

Soon after the reading, I was pleased to find at least a few other people who were starting to explore alternative spiritual paths. Most of them shared my disillusionment with the traditional church. For whatever reasons, the church hadn't worked for us, and we were looking to other forms of spiritual expression.

I didn't get involved with any particular group or course of study, and I didn't do anything that would be considered extreme—yet. I just went on with my life at work and at home, but I found myself becoming more interested in spiritual things. I began to ask a lot of questions.

In late December, my girlfriend Kari and I went to Big Sur for New Year's. It was a last-minute decision, and we had no specific plans except to be in an especially beautiful place for the beginning of the new year. We had picked Big Sur because it was one of the most spectacular places on the California coast.

We drove past Monterey and Carmel and down Highway I through the Redwoods and into Big Sur. We stopped at the Nepenthe Bookstore, which towered over a particularly scenic stretch of the coastline. While in the bookstore, I felt led to buy a book called *Journey Towards the Heart*, by an Indian master named Bhagwan Shree Rajneesh. I felt a little strange purchasing a book by someone described as a guru, but I bought it anyway.

When I paid for the book, I asked the cashier to recommend a place where we could spend the night. "Deetjen's" was his quick reply. He said the old resort was unique and reasonably priced. But he warned me that the owner was rather eccentric and had to like you before he'd give you a room. The cashier smiled and said we would have to take our chances but that we would probably be okay.

I thanked him for the help, and we followed his directions to head south a bit on Highway 1. And then, just as he had described, on the left was the old resort and the sign saying "Deetjen." A number of rustic wooden cabins were nestled in and around the base of a very steep hill. A man walked out into the parking lot to meet us. He seemed to be the owner, and I did feel him giving me a long look before he told us he had a room. After Kari and I picked out the cabin we liked, I felt him studying me again.

"How would you like to stay on top of this mountain tonight?" he suddenly asked.

I was taken by surprise, but I said, "Sure, why not?" The top of a mountain seemed a great place to be on New Year's Eve—especially in Big Sur.

He told me to park the car, get whatever we would need for the night, and register inside. A man named Orion would meet us outside in ten minutes and drive us up the mountain. Then without another word, he turned and walked away.

Inside the office, I told the desk clerk that we would be staying on top of the mountain. I was surprised when she did a quick double-take. "You're staying at Tophouse?" Her tone implied that being asked to stay there was unusual, and quite the honor, especially on New Year's Eve.

After completing the registration, I thanked her, paid for the room, and went outside with Kari. Orion picked us up, and soon we were on our way up the mountain. What an adventure! Here we were in Big Sur on New Year's Eve with a book by an Indian guru in my pack, a guy named Orion driving us up a mountain road toward a mysterious place called Tophouse, and the sun setting in the west.

As we wound our way up the mountain road, the colors of the year's final sunset flashed and flickered through the trees. In the distance was the Pacific Ocean. I had to ask myself, *Is this really happening?*

Even with the dramatic build-up, we had no idea just how incredible it would be when we reached the top. When we got out of the car, we looked straight out to blue sky and straight down to a continuous cloud bank that blanketed the sky from horizon to horizon. We felt as if we were standing on top of the world. If it wasn't heaven on earth, it had to be close.

After saying good-bye to Orion, who had taken us to our room, Kari and I stood at the little window looking out at the horizon and down at the clouds. It was like a room in the sky, floating above the world, frozen in time and suspended in space. A tremendous stillness enveloped us. We had found ourselves in the middle of a dream. It had to be one of the most beautiful places I had ever been in my life.

And it was in the perfection of that moment that I saw the book on the night stand next to the bed—*Only One Sky*, by Bhagwan Shree Rajneesh! What were the odds? A man I had never heard of before today—and now here was a second book by him. Bhagwan Shree Rajneesh. Who was this mystery man?

I looked again at the book that lay there with such apparent innocence, imagining that Rajneesh himself was watching. Journey Towards the Heart at Nepenthe. *Only One Sky* here at Top-house. The two Rajneesh titles were the literal bookends of an amazing journey from Highway 1 to the top of this mountain. Cosmic coincidence or meaningless chance? Putting the books aside for the moment, I settled in with Kari, and we had a quiet and wonderfully peaceful New Year's Eve.

The next morning I started reading *Only One Sky*. Once I began the book, it was difficult to put down. Rajneesh was a breath of fresh air; he told stories, cracked jokes, and gently confronted me with my shortcomings. He was unsparingly straightforward and knowledgeable as he talked about all sorts of spiritual things. And he wasn't afraid of tackling the hypocrisy of traditional religion. I found myself immediately charmed by this unpredictable Indian mystic whose almost messianic message was that we surrender the ego. He cut to the core, and I was deeply moved. At times I could feel his words reaching inside me and connecting with the spiritually starved part of me that Bonnie had described in my reading.

As I read page after page, I seemed to fall deeper and deeper inside myself. It was as if Rajneesh had thrown a master switch in the depths of my soul. His spiritual presence seemed to flood my being, and as it did I could feel a warmth and softness of spirit that had been missing for years. My previously unexpressed spiritual needs were suddenly being attended to by this man Rajneesh. He seemed to know me better than I knew myself. His thoughts and ideas and beliefs were like my own. For the first time since I was a young boy, I was actually excited about God.

I wasn't aware of having held anything against God all these years, but I had definitely put Him on hold while I had gone on with the business of living my life. But here in Big Sur, high above the ocean on this miraculous mountain, reading this book, I could feel something spiritual moving into my life.

As Kari and I got ready to leave later in the morning, we stood in the yard looking out at the ocean. As we took in the magnificent view one last time, it was hard to believe that my mountaintop experience could be anything less than a benign and divine supernatural set-up to point me toward Rajneesh, who was now pointing me

toward God. As we finally turned to go, I sensed that my introduction to Rajneesh was the beginning of what would be a most
unusual spiritual journey.

2

Back in Berkeley a few days later, I stopped by a metaphysical
bookstore to see if I could find any more books by Rajneesh.
I had never been in a metaphysical bookstore before and was fascinated that a store could be wholly devoted to spiritual subjects—
everything from the secret teachings of the masters of the Far East
to the mysteries of astral projection, from discovering past lives to
kundalini yoga—shelf after shelf of astrology, reincarnation, psychic
healing, and other related subjects. It was in the Eastern section that
I found the books by Rajneesh. I was already feeling compelled to
read anything I could find by him. In fact, I was getting so caught
up with Rajneesh that I didn't know if I was seeking him or he was
seeking me. Rajneesh had pushed me into the river, but he was beyond trying to teach me how to swim. Instead, he was showing me
how to go with the flow.

As I stood in the middle of the bookstore, I suddenly became
aware of the most extraordinary music. It was a beautiful, haunt-
ing melody with a soft, lyrical, almost meditative refrain. The music
seemed to penetrate my entire being as it merged with the feelings
that had already been inspired by Rajneesh. I felt a happy kind of
sadness that seemed to have something to do with a longing for
God.

Walking over to the woman who was working in the store, I
asked, "Who is playing that incredible music?"

She handed me the empty jacket of an album called "Haleakala,"
by a man named Chaitanya Hari Deuter. When I flipped the album
cover over I was stunned to see a color photograph of Rajneesh, and
under it Deuter had written the following words:

> I gratefully dedicate this record to my master Bhagwan
> Shree Rajneesh.

I could hardly believe it. Rajneesh was everywhere.

In that moment I *really* got it. Rajneesh was here to be my teacher. I had asked for help, and help had been sent. Rajneesh would be the one to help me find God. That was what a guru was all about. Needless to say, I bought the album.

3

Hot on the trail, I tracked down a Rajneesh Center in San Francisco and went to it. Full of enthusiasm and loaded with questions, I knocked on the door. I was still somewhat surprised by my excitement about a guru. Following gurus had always seemed to be a cop-out to me—so mindless and empty. Now here I was suddenly fascinated by a guru who was convincing me that to spiritually grow I needed to become *more* mindless and empty. And it made sense.

The Rajneesh followers I met at the Center were bright and energetic. Although their orange clothing seemed a bit strange, I knew it was done in some kind of obedience to Rajneesh, and I respected it as such. I found in them an openness and spontaneity that I desired for myself, qualities that had to come from what they had learned from Rajneesh.

But as much as I liked the "sannyasins," I was also intimidated by them. I knew that many of them had been with Rajneesh in India, living in the ashram and doing groups and workshops. I was impressed by their commitment to go half-way around the world in their search for truth and that they had found their truth in the person of Rajneesh. He was the gate his sannyasins passed through in their surrender to God.

I told the sannyasins how Rajneesh had suddenly appeared in my life and that I was still trying to understand what it all meant and where I should go from here. When I said that Rajneesh kept popping up in strange places, there were knowing glances and lots of laughter. They eagerly shared their own experiences of how Rajneesh had approached them in similarly remarkable and mysterious ways. He seemed to call his followers to him. One of the sannyasins looked at me and smiled and said that it probably wouldn't be long before I was off to India to become a sannyasin myself.

After talking about Rajneesh and India at length, the sannyasins gave me information on books, workshops, meditations, Sufi dancing, and other activities, even a newsletter from India. And as I was leaving, one of them told me that two sannyasins lived in my town. Their names were Dharmananda and Veena, and he gave me their number.

Three

Zorba the Buddha

When I arrived back home, one of the first things I did was to call Dharmananda and Veena. I talked with Veena and told her of my interest in Rajneesh and my eagerness to meet with them. She said she was glad I had called and that one of them would get in touch with me soon about setting something up. They definitely would like to get together.

When Dharmananda called back and invited me to their house for "a meditation," I quickly accepted. I was excited about being included in a meditation. I knew from my reading that Rajneesh considered meditation to be one of the keys to enlightenment and that he encouraged his followers to meditate often. He had even created special meditations for his followers, and Dharmananda said that we would be doing one of those meditations when we got together.

As I sat in my living room thinking about my upcoming get-together with Dharmananda and Veena and my involvement with Rajneesh, I had to laugh. Rajneesh was not the kind of person I would have purposely gone out looking for, but it was becoming clear that there was unpredictability and mystery in the pursuit of a spiritual life. And I was happy that my suspicion, even disdain, for guru figures had vanished once I understood what they were all about. It was almost unbelievable that I had gone from being so spiritually close-minded to following a guru in a matter of months. The gradual, step-by-step process had helped me get past my unwarranted resistance to spiritual things.

The big breakthrough, of course, had been my acquaintance with Kay. She had helped me overcome my lifelong suspicion of psychics and metaphysical teachings. And she had prepared the way for my appointment with Bonnie. In the reading itself, Bonnie had been credible. I had liked her and trusted her, and she had "seen" into my life. And then, of course, the unexpected ball of light—the other side's dramatic way of saying hello and offering me help. My confidence in that supernatural experience prompted me to pray to those on the other side for their help. And then the remarkable synchronistic events when Rajneesh mysteriously bypassed my rational mind amidst the splendor of Big Sur and moved magically into my life. And my surprisingly quick and easy acceptance of him because it was clear that it was meant to be.

I was grateful for all that was happening. I was grateful to Kay, to Bonnie, and to the other side for their obvious interest in me, and to Rajneesh, who was taking me deeper and deeper into the mysteries of spiritual life. My feet were now planted on a spiritual path—the path of Rajneesh. The old saying was true—that when the student is ready, the teacher appears. I had announced my readiness in my rooftop prayer, but I had no idea that my help would come in the form of an offbeat, paradoxical Indian guru.

I was not only accepting Rajneesh but also becoming devoted to him and his idiosyncratic spiritual ways. I knew that most of the world would see him as weird, but I found him enlightening as he talked about that same condemning world in no uncertain terms. He saw through its phoniness and flattery and two-dimensionality. He saw through the hypocrisy of its religions that depended on doctrine and dogma and words from a book. Rajneesh was refreshing; he exposed a world that was locked into its own intellectuality and couldn't make the jump from its head to its heart. I respected his confrontational nature. He seemed to be a spiritual straight-shooter in an age of church double-talk. And although some might regard Rajneesh as a cult figure or even a spiritual clown, I saw him as a radical teacher with a radical message, who delivered it with the wit and wisdom and irony of the classic Shakespearean fool. But I knew that only those who were open enough to see past the Western stereotype of an Indian guru would understand the importance of his message.

If they were open enough, people would see that Rajneesh's teachings were a masterful distillation of all the great religious teachers—Buddha, Mohammed, Jesus, Lao-Tzu, Confucius. He had a genius for fine-tuning their teachings and representing them in his own unique and inimitable way. The more I read Rajneesh, the more I understood that the message of the Buddha was the same as Mohammed's and the message of Jesus the same as Lao-Tzu's. Each master had his own way of presenting what was really the same truth.

Rajneesh pointed out that each master had his own devices. He was going to do whatever was necessary to push, pull, or shock sannyasins out of their illusions into awareness. His goal was to teach his followers that truth is the totality of all apparent contradiction and paradox, and in that totality or wholeness is the oneness of all religions. In that oneness, the universal truths underlying the world's religions could be found.

I was learning that masters such as Jesus and Buddha and Lao-Tzu, and now Rajneesh, were teaching the one truth that God is everywhere and in everyone and in everything. He exists inside our very selves, waiting to be sought and found, but we ironically go here and there and all over the world seeking a God that is already inside us waiting to be discovered. I was learning that our journey is not an outward journey but, rather, inward into the vast realms of our divine consciousness. Our only obstacles are our own self-imposed limitations. As we shed our false beliefs of a sinful self we can more fully appreciate and love ourselves for who we are—a glorious part of the totality and oneness and perfection that we call God.

It seemed incredibly simple yet hard to realize. I was beginning to understand why a spiritual master such as Rajneesh was necessary. We need someone who knows what is going on to lead us through the maze of our own confusion, back to the simplicity and source of it all, back to ourselves and to our oneness with God.

The guru's job is always to turn the disciple back toward himself or herself, to teach us the bottom line that each of us is "the way, the truth, and the life." Only as we let go of our spiritual misconceptions, worldly preoccupations, and tyrannical egos can we get in touch with our innate connection to the oneness of God.

2

The next week I went to Dharmananda and Veena's house. Both brightly dressed in sannyasin attire, they greeted me warmly. As they ushered me into their living room, they informed me that at least one other person would be joining our meditation. Dharmananda and Veena talked animatedly of Rajneesh and India. They glowed as they talked of the encounters, the growth groups, the meditations, and Rajneesh's avant-garde approach to spirituality. He was attracting some of the most innovative men and women in the human potential movement—powerful, spiritually challenging, and even intimidating men such as Teertha, who was now second in command. Rajneesh was also attracting doctors, lawyers, business executives, and a cross-section of highly motivated, educated seekers who were giving up everything to come to India and be with him.

Dharmananda described how Rajneesh had created an amazing blend of psychotherapy, bodywork and spiritual discipline that had become, in effect, a new dynamic transpersonal growth process. People all over the world were cutting through layers of lifelong hang-ups and emotional blocks through his teachings, meditations, and growth groups. They were choosing to let go of the guilt, anger, and hurt from their past so that they could be more fully alive in the present. They were learning to decide how they would feel by consciously *responding* from their hearts rather than unconsciously reacting from habitual behavior patterns based on old hurts.

I asked many questions about the growth groups, the meditations, and life in India, and when we finally concluded our discussion we agreed that Rajneesh was a most wonderful and unusual spiritual teacher. In his devious, devilish way he was presenting ancient truths in an entirely new light. We knew that in his world of monks with firecrackers, cryptic Sufi mystics, and kings with magic rings, he was teaching us about life, love, and God.

We all agreed that Rajneesh was a true man of mystery. Charming, confrontational, and brilliantly extemporaneous, he could turn what looked like an off-color joke about the pope into a spiritual lesson. He truly made life a celebrative happening—never dull or dry. And for those of us sitting in the room, he had made our lives much more worthwhile through his teachings. Thanks to Rajneesh, we were moving away from the world and the life of the "Nowhere Man" and more toward the Rajneesh ideal of "Zorba the Buddha." That is, one who could enter deeply into the mystery of God and oneness while also celebrating life with outrageous abandon. One who sees nothing but God and celebrates that awareness in every waking moment.

After talking for an hour or so about Rajneesh and India and the challenges of seeking truth, Dharmananda said it was time for the meditation. He led us outside past their samadhi tank and swimming pool to the meditation room. He said we would be doing one of the Rajneesh meditations from India specifically designed to wear down and eventually relax the Western mind. He described the stages of the meditation, which blended vigorous physical activity with stillness and silence. He said we would all wear blindfolds to enhance the process of going within and that a special tape would lead us through the various stages of the meditation. He made it clear that the essential purpose of the meditation was to learn to let go.

The lights went out. The blindfolds went on. Suddenly I was moving and shaking to the staccato beat of Indian drums. I twisted and turned and gyrated amidst the grunts and groans of the others in the room. For a moment the apparent insanity of what I was doing hit me head-on. Here I was, with people I had known a little more than an hour, in a dark room with a blindfold on, shaking and swaying madly to this frantic Indian music. It seemed utterly absurd.

But those thoughts quickly subsided as my body seemed to take off on its own, rocking and reverberating and responding to the chaotic rhythms. I could feel myself fully entering into the meditation, and my involvement continued throughout the various stages so that by the time we reached the climactic period of silence, I was so completely relaxed that the line separating me from the meditation was gone. In that moment, I realized that the meditation and I had become mysteriously one. It was yet another gift from Rajneesh—an understanding that my divine connection was really present.

When I said good-bye that night to my new Rajneesh friends, I had to smile as I thought about the evening. I recognized that it was the stuff "Saturday Night Live" was made of, but I knew that what I was doing was helping me. And besides, no one had ever told me that spiritual life could be so exciting and fun.

In the coming days, I did the Rajneesh meditations daily. And within a matter of weeks, I had opened a special savings account with the code name Poona. I was determined to go to Poona, India to be with Rajneesh.

I continued to get together with Dharmananda and Veena. They shared their Rajneesh tapes, told me stories about India, and encouraged me in my spiritual pursuits. One of the things I really liked about my new friends was that they were unwilling to compromise themselves by simply adapting to the world. They wanted more from life than a nine-to-five job and a color TV. They had a consuming desire to be genuine and authentic people.

3

Several months into my Rajneesh phenomenon, Kari came up from Berkeley for a visit. As she looked through a recent issue of *Sannyas Magazine,* which I was now receiving directly from India, she became concerned as she saw the pictures of sannyasin women. She thought it would be only a matter of time before I fell for one of them. I was getting so carried away by Rajneesh and his sannyasins that she was afraid I would leave her behind.

She wasn't presenting an ultimatum, but I could read between the lines. I knew that if I didn't do something, she would eventually leave in self-defense. In the panic of the moment I couldn't imagine her not being in my life. Later that afternoon, I told her how important she was to me. I told her that I didn't want her to leave me and that I would put Rajneesh out of my life. I meant what I said, but I didn't have any idea at the time how difficult that would be.

Often on weekends I made the three-hour drive to the Bay Area to be with Kari. We would take walks, go out to eat, and watch movies on TV. But it didn't work. As much as I cared about her, I could still feel the spiritual vacuum left in my life by my abandonment of Rajneesh. Because I had compromised my spirituality, I now felt empty and even a little depressed. I had maintained the relationship with Kari, but cutting off Rajneesh cold turkey had been a deathblow to my spirit.

My way of countering the emptiness and depression was to take an extended leave of absence from work to travel in Hawaii. I knew I needed to shake free from my spiritual stagnation, and I thought a new environment might help. At the last moment Kari decided to come along for the first two weeks of my trip, but she had to return to the Bay Area while I stayed in the islands for another month or two. She wasn't too thrilled about my being in

Hawaii by myself for that length of time, but she was resigned to my need to get away.

Almost as soon as we arrived on the island of Maui, Kari got sick. After descending from the top of Mount Haleakala, she got an earache that wouldn't go away. We stopped at a local health food store, hoping to find something that would help. As we looked around the store, I happened to see a notice on the bulletin board that Indian master Baba Hari Das would be speaking that night at the Maui Community College. Kari noticed my obvious interest.

Back at the little motel that afternoon, she was feeling so bad that she could barely talk. It was hardly the way to spend a vacation. I was surprised when she managed a smile and told me to go see the guru at the college. She said that I needed to get out of the room for a while and that she knew how much I wanted to go. I was glad she felt okay about my going, and I was on my way to see him an hour later.

4

The overflow crowd at the college was expectant and eager, and it felt good to be in a place that had such a strong spiritual presence. Baba Hari Das was "in silence." He wrote down answers to questions from the audience, which were then read aloud by his assistant. It was an unusual format, to say the least, but it seemed to add to the ambience of the evening. The Indian guru's dialogue was sprinkled with all sorts of Eastern wisdom, and I was much in accord with what he was saying.

In the middle of his presentation, my eyes caught a flash of orange color across the room, immediately locking in on a man in sannyasin attire. I felt a surge of adrenalin as I reconnected with the feelings I still had for Rajneesh. The image of that sannyasin and the feeling of spiritual community in that room stayed with me for the rest of the night. I felt as if something had been pried open deep in my spirit. And I knew that the reawakening of my spiritual life was too important to my well-being to shut down ever again.

The next day in downtown Wailuku, Kari and I were in a bookstore where I suddenly found myself standing in front of a book by Rajneesh. Almost at once, I could feel the mysterious, magnetic pull as I picked up the book about Patanjali's Sutras. Funny that I should be confronted with this book right after seeing a guru and a Rajneesh sannyasin. I had tried to distance myself from Rajneesh, but it hadn't worked. He still had an enormous hold on my life, and I could feel it as I stood there glancing through his book.

Moments later, I saw the flyer on the wall in front of me: Let-Go Intensive. Kona Light Center. Big Island, Hawaii. Led by Swami Anand Alok from Maneisha Rajneesh Center, Oahu. I guess by that point I shouldn't have been surprised. The trapdoor had been thrown open, and Rajneesh was back in my life. As I stood staring at the flyer, I knew that resisting Rajneesh was impossible and that my involvement with the irrepressible guru not only was *meant* to be but *had* to be. What amazed me was that the workshop was to begin within several days of my already scheduled arrival on the Big Island of Hawaii. I could hardly believe it.

Impulsively, I told Kari about the workshop and that I had seen the flyer immediately after looking at a Rajneesh book. I told her that I was going to buy the book and sign up for the workshop. With quiet resignation, she managed the tiniest of smiles. There wasn't much she could say. Still sick, disappointed in the trip, and now disillusioned with me, she slowly started to retreat within herself.

Several days later as we sat in a Japanese restaurant in Lahaina looking at our menus, she started crying. She didn't make a sound, but the tears just kept coming. She knew what I was too selfish or blind to see—that when she flew out of the Maui airport in a few days, we would never see each other again. Our romance was over.

She knew my feelings for her were strong, but my commitment to Rajneesh was stronger. In that moment, she realized that I was not the one who would be there for her. She was smart to get out when she did.

5

I had phoned ahead to the Kona Light Center from Maui and made my reservation for the Let-Go Workshop. Arriving at the Kona airport, I ended up hitching a ride with a Jeepful of sannyasins all the way to the Light Center, and I was off and running on another adventure. As we drove past downtown Kona and up the long hill to the Center, I looked out at the immense expanse of ocean surrounding the island. There was a quiet calm on the Big Island that felt spiritual. I was glad to be there with the sannyasins. One of them remarked on the providential timing of my trip to Kona, and jokes were made about Bhagwan and how he reeled in his sannyasins in the strangest ways. Like other sannyasins I had met, they were already predicting that I would end up in India.

The Kona Light Center sat on a hill that looked straight out onto the Pacific Ocean. It was a beautiful place for a workshop. And the little room I was staying in had a stark Eastern simplicity that added to the overall spiritual feel. I was very happy to be back on the path of Rajneesh.

The workshop started on Friday night. It was led by Alok, a sannyasin who had spent extensive time in India. But the group almost ended as soon as it began for me. I left the group after a particularly difficult initial exercise that brought up so many feelings of self-consciousness and unworthiness that I broke down crying. I fled to my room at the break and collapsed in a dark corner. I was overcome with feelings of self-disgust. I wasn't spiritual, and I never would be. I couldn't even do the introductory encounter. *Who am I kidding?* I thought. *I'll just fly back to the Bay Area and forget the whole thing—Rajneesh and all.*

Panna, the tall, spiritually radiant co-leader of the group, came to my room and found me sitting in the dark. She said, "Come back to the group. We are all waiting for you."

I summoned what dignity I had left and told her, "Panna, I can't go back to the group. If I do, I will probably be in tears the whole weekend."

Then she did the most amazing thing. She walked over to me and, putting her hand on my forehead and smiling broadly, said in the most compassionate and loving tone, "Wouldn't it be wonderful if you could!"

Her permission to be whatever I was feeling helped me, and suddenly it didn't matter that I wasn't strong or that I felt inadequate or cried. It didn't matter because I felt cared for, and in that moment I knew it was okay to be me—whoever me was. My feelings of desperation had been gently wiped away. Panna accompanied me back to the group, and it turned out to be an important weekend of facing fears, expressing sadness, meditating, and learning to let go. I opened up in all sorts of ways.

After the weekend, a couple in the group invited me to stay at their house, which was on the ocean in a picturesque fishing village. I was still high from the group, and I spent the next several days swimming, meditating, and reading Rajneesh. I felt different and wondered what had been touched so deeply inside me. I knew it had something to do with entrusting myself to a group of people who were highly committed to personal and spiritual growth. They knew that they had hang-ups, too, and were willing to talk about them and work on them. I found it interesting that even the most mellow and seemingly self-confident group members had deep-seated issues they were trying to work out in their lives. It was only after we had all dropped the facade that everything was okay in our lives that we had made real heart-to-heart connections. And, of course, in the backdrop of our conversations and encounters was the spirit of Rajneesh. It was comforting to know that he would work with us and help us in our spiritual struggles. We were not alone. We had Rajneesh, and we had each other.

After a few days in the fishing village, I took off on a trip around the island with a woman who was also living in my new friend's house. She, too, was interested in Rajneesh and spiritual things. For a week or so, we drove around the Big Island walking the beaches, exploring the countryside, and reading Rajneesh. We fed the giant goldfish in downtown Hilo, did puppet shows from the car window, and had a crazy, wonderful time. She was like a continuation of the workshop for me, as she refused to let me take myself seriously. Somehow Rajneesh, the workshop, and now this friend had given me a new sense of identity. I was finally starting to feel good about myself, even like myself. It was a most unusual feeling.

One evening as my new friend and I sat in a little Italian restaurant outside Hilo, we plotted our escape to India. We would become sannyasins and adopt new names. Through our surrender to Rajneesh we would become the people we knew we could be.

6

When my Hawaiian journey finally came to an end, I flew back to the mainland. It was late as I drove through San Francisco and over the Golden Gate Bridge to my old college roommate's house in the Marin hills. As I wound my way through the outskirts of Mill Valley, I could feel how much I had changed during the months in Hawaii. But I was also thinking of Kari and had an empty feeling inside as I thought about the phone call when she'd told me that our relationship was over. It was strange to think I wouldn't see her any more, but I knew that was how it had to be because I was firmly committed to my ongoing journey with Rajneesh.

Once home, I started to wear various shades of orange in my clothing. At first it was an orange shirt or orange tie-dyed pants, but it wasn't long before I was wearing orange everything. I even wore orange socks. It was my most extreme move to date and was obvious evidence of my growing commitment to Rajneesh. It was also proof that my outward identification with Rajneesh and his sannyasins was now stronger than my self-consciousness of how I was being perceived. I was devoted to Rajneesh and his teachings, and I was inching closer and closer to becoming a sannyasin.

During that time, I also moved my desk out of my office and built a new one so that I could sit on the floor. I hung a picture of Rajneesh over the desk and enclosed my entire work area in a wall of bamboo screens. Co-workers would come in and meditate with me on breaks, and I was fast becoming known as the resident "yogi."

Sometimes I would catch the eyes of the State Farm Insurance agents that worked next door as they passed my window and saw me sitting on my pillow, dressed in orange and doing my paperwork or talking on the phone. I could feel them studying me and surveying my mini ashram. They probably thought that I had gone completely out of my mind.

Four

Joy in My Life

After my trip to Hawaii, my spirituality had definitely resurfaced, and once again it became the predominant focus of my life. I did the Rajneesh "dynamic meditation" almost daily. The deep feeling of relaxation that I got from it was a great way to start the day. When I wasn't busy at work, I would immerse myself in a new book or article from the ever-increasing pile of Rajneesh literature I was accumulating.

By this time, I had grown particularly fond of the stories and parables that Rajneesh wove throughout his writings. He could convey complex spiritual truths through the simplest of stories. I believed that Rajneesh understood life; he had a grasp on what was and wasn't true. In my mind he was a master teacher, and I knew that he was helping me to reorient myself to God by realigning me both spiritually and psychologically. It was a painful process to try to come to grips with who I was, but with my new metaphysical tools and understandings I was learning to be honest with myself. And I was also learning to communicate effectively what I was feeling—not just what I thought other people wanted to hear.

In dealing with myself in a spiritually disciplined way, I was also beginning to feel myself opening up in new ways. The accepting, nonjudgmental attitude of Rajneesh and his sannyasins provided me with a safe and secure environment as I tried to work through the issues that were surfacing for me. And in that environment of acceptance and loving confrontation, I knew that I was really starting to grow spiritually.

2

Then I met Joy. I was introduced to her at a local cafe by a mutual friend. She was radiant that night, and I could sense her strong spiritual nature. I liked her right away.

Joy and I continued to cross paths in the coming days. When we did, our conversations always carried a strong spiritual thrust. We were both committed to our spiritual lives, and I soon realized that as a seeker she was my female counterpart. We both wanted to learn more about ourselves and to get past the multitude of inner obstacles that kept us from having relationships with God and others. Our mutual enthusiasm for spiritual things became the foundation of our friendship.

Whenever we met on the street or in a restaurant or at the university we were glad to see each other. It was as if we were lifelong friends, and we talked with great excitement about whatever was happening in our lives. At gatherings we would gravitate toward each other, usually ending up in a corner sharing our latest thoughts and spiritual insights. Oblivious to others, we would discuss the ups and downs of our spiritual adventures. We talked animatedly about our dreams, the books we were reading, and all the little synchronistic happenings that made life interesting. We took advantage of every opportunity to share our love of spiritual things.

Joy, I found out quickly, was extremely intuitive. When I would bump into her unexpectedly, she would say, "I knew that I was going to see you today!" When I spontaneously stopped by her house, she would greet me saying, "I knew you were coming over." I was both baffled and impressed by her ability to intuit and perceive things before they happened.

Joy told me she had been somewhat psychic since about the age of thirteen and that she'd had some out-of-body experiences as well as being involved with a host of other things, including a recent fascination with Indian guru Swami Baba Muktananda. I thought it extremely interesting that she had also been involved with a guru, and we spent hours talking about the insights we had gained from our respective Indian teachers.

I began to understand that Joy had what she called her "spiritual process." It was a progressive, cumulative spiritual growth that was always changing and evolving. I was a little mystified at times by Joy and her "process," but I watched her with ever-increasing respect. Her commitment to knowing herself and knowing God was all-consuming. She had an inner drive that was almost relentless, and it pushed her higher and higher toward truth and God.

As time went on, I watched Joy move in and out of various spiritual things. She wasn't flighty or haphazard. There was always an exact timing and purpose to what she participated in, and she always seemed to extract the essence from whatever it was she was doing. She also left behind whatever was not meaningful or valuable. Each spiritual experience would peak and naturally subside and slide into the next activity.

Our friendship was unique in that we were not romantically involved. When mutual friends would suggest that we made a great couple, we were quick to point out that we were "only friends." The fact that we were not romantically involved freed us up considerably to be friends. We were able to get to know each other without the sexual undertones that so often characterize and monopolize the early stages of a new relationship. Instead, we became each other's own support group, bringing mutual encouragement to each other in all that we did. It seemed strange to others that we devoted so much of our time to spiritual concerns, but to us it was the most natural thing in the world. We both wanted to get past ourselves and find whatever truth was out there. And we were both willing to do whatever we had to do to find it. Everything else in our lives paled next to our spiritual quest.

3

Shortly after the new year, I went to a Rajneesh Let-Go intensive at Harbin Hot Springs, which was about a three-hour drive from my home and not far from the Napa Valley. Amitabh, a gifted sannyasin who had been a highly respected Rajneesh group leader in India, led the weekend workshop. The two days were intense and filled with meditations, personal encounters, group process, dancing, and a special healing time in Harbin's hot mineral waters. When emotional areas were opened up in meditation, we were encouraged to "work on" those various personal concerns.

The group was supportive and accepting, and people had a chance to deal with things that were bothering them. Some people came to the workshop with specific issues. Amitabh was sensitive and intuitive and usually worked with an individual one-on-one but always in the context of the group. He facilitated interactions between people, suggested certain role playing, and knew when it was time to stop working with one person and move on to another. A lot of healing took place in the group, and over the course of the weekend there was a growing feeling of closeness and community as we openly shared and worked on our problems together.

On one of our breaks, we were all dancing in a big sunny room to Bob Dylan's recent *Slow Train* album. We were happy that Dylan was now on the spiritual path, and we felt a camaraderie and celebrative abandon as we rocked out to his song "Gotta Serve Somebody."

> Well, it may be the devil or it may be the Lord
> But you're gonna have to serve somebody.

Dylan's words seemed to fill the room as we moved and grooved in a state of mellow semi-bliss. Connecting more with Dylan, rather than with what he was saying, most of his lyrics went flying right past us.

All in all, the workshop proved to be healing for me, and by the end of the weekend we were all feeling relaxed as we headed back into the world.

4

That Monday I was still extremely high from the weekend. When several co-workers pressed me for details about the workshop, I was glad to tell them about it. I remember feeling very spiritual as I recounted the meditations and heavy discussions. Whether I admitted it or not, it was important to me that I be perceived by others as a spiritual person. In a way it was a new identity for me, and it made me feel good.

Toward the end of the week, I could feel the glow of the weekend wearing off. I wished the warmth and fellowship could stay with me forever. But the good feelings seemed to slip away. Needless to say, I was elated to learn there would be another Harbin weekend in a month. I immediately sent in my $100 registration fee and looked forward to the workshop for days in advance.

By now the people in my office were getting used to my unorthodox spiritual ways. Although a number of them seemed to enjoy hearing about my spiritual adventures, one woman seemed concerned and gave me a Bible. She urged me to read it. I was glad she had something that made her happy, but I knew that her old-fashioned brand of spirituality was not what I wanted. Christianity was so outdated for these tremendously exciting spiritual times. I wished she would get real and come to a Rajneesh weekend where she could dance and shout and meditate and process her feelings—she'd never go back to church.

5

When I walked in the door of the second Harbin workshop, I felt as if I had come home. Familiar faces from the last workshop lit up when I arrived, and there were hugs all around.

Within minutes, I was embraced by the warmth and affection that characterized the Rajneesh groups. A caring and love underlined everything we did. I felt safe and supported by these people in orange.

Rajneesh intensives gave many of us who were spiritually isolated a feeling of family. We had a sense of community, and, as always, behind everything was the presence of Rajneesh. He was the binding force, the motivator, the teacher of us all.

But I noted that my respect and devotion to Rajneesh had its limits. I pulled back a bit when sannyasins sat in front of his picture and worshiped him. As much as I cared about Rajneesh and saw him as an incredible part of God, I could not begin to see him as God. My struggle in that area made my surrendering to him almost impossible. I could surrender to his teachings but not to him. And I knew that was one reason I had not already flown to India and become a sannyasin. I wasn't sure I wanted to hand my life over to him that way. He could be my master teacher but not my master. Rajneesh was always chiding those of us who remained on the periphery of his energy without completely committing our lives to God through him. I knew in my heart that I had no problem surrendering my life to God, but I trusted my hesitancy and honored my reluctance to worship Rajneesh.

After suffering an unusual illness, I was shocked one day to realize that my preoccupation with Rajneesh was gone. The spiritual electricity that had charged my relationship with him was no longer there. I didn't like it, and I didn't understand. It was almost as if my strong feelings for Rajneesh had left with my illness.

I was so troubled by my change of heart that I spent nearly a week trying to resurrect my lost zeal—but to no avail. The thrill was definitely gone. The sheer joy I had once experienced with Rajneesh had been reduced almost overnight to the detached respect reserved for a former teacher. No matter how much I tried to revive it, the spiritual romance was over.

I tried to analyze what had happened, but it was no use. Was I too scared to go to India? Did my inability to see Rajneesh as God subconsciously do me in? Or was it simply time for a change? I didn't know, but the shift was so sudden and extreme that it caught me completely by surprise. There was nothing conscious about it. The Rajneesh mystique was gone.

So, as Joy had done with her guru Muktananda, I found myself sidestepping Rajneesh. I was grateful for all that he had taught me and would definitely take his teachings with me in my heart, but I could not continue with him. Something else was around the bend. Maybe my intense relationship with him would return again someday. Maybe it wouldn't. Difficult as it was to comprehend, Rajneesh was out for now.

6

In the wake of my missing mystical preoccupation with Rajneesh, I decided to visit a local psychic named Carolyn, who came highly recommended by a friend at work. Maybe she would pick up the spiritual slack I was feeling and provide some direction for my spiritual journey.

On my first visit she impressed me with the precision and range of things she knew about me. She made many helpful suggestions, and I decided to see her on a semi-regular basis. At the end of each session, Carolyn gave me the typewritten outline of the reading, which she had psychically prepared the night before. At the end of the sheet there was always a recommended book to read and an affirmation especially appropriate for that week.

Affirmations were designed to encourage certain positive thoughts and to reinforce particular metaphysical teachings. They often reminded me of my own inner perfection and inherently divine nature. They were like shields of truth to use against arrows of negativity and illusion that shot into my mind from incorrect thinking.

The affirmations had the feel of prayers, but they were really inspiration and encouragement from me to myself. Terms such as *divine love* and *divine mind* were common. I usually felt great comfort and encouragement as I repeated, "I am divine love" or "My mind is a part of the divine mind."

I could see that Carolyn's readings and teachings were consistent with what I had already been taught by Bonnie and Rajneesh. They were all saying the same thing, and everything was now fitting neatly into what was becoming my metaphysical world view. I immediately read the books that Carolyn recommended. The first book was U. S. Anderson's *Three Magic Words*. Kept in suspense until the end of the book, I learned that the three magic words were "I am God." It was another brush stroke applied to my metaphysical picture. Bonnie had given me my introduction, Rajneesh had given me an eloquent and poetic schematic, and now Carolyn was helping me fill in some of the remaining areas.

As one teacher reinforced the teachings of another, I began to appreciate and understand the consistency of the spiritual principles that now governed my life. I saw more and more of the interconnectedness and oneness of life. I was perfect and whole and divinely connected to the universal mind, and the more I saw myself and others as perfect, the more my life would change. Finally, I was learning to live in the light of my own divine being, the light that was God and also me.

Sometimes when I was alone, images of my spiritual journey would flash through my mind: psychic readings, a ball of light, my rooftop prayer, a room in the sky in Big Sur, a hip Indian guru, the Let-Go group in Hawaii, the Harbin Hot Springs intensives, and the meditations with blindfolded people in orange. It seemed crazy and outrageous, yet somehow it all made sense.

I felt like an explorer in a new, exciting frontier. More and more people were going to psychics, learning to meditate, and seeing that they could create their own reality. We were finally learning that God was everywhere and in everyone and that we were all one. This new frontier and growing movement was gathering momentum. And as I reflected on some of the spiritual shifts and changes that were making inroads into the American consciousness, I had to smile at the irony. It used to be a put-down when we were kids to say, "Who do you think you are? God?" Now we were learning that we were putting ourselves down if we didn't answer that question with a resounding "Yes!" It was the spiritual equivalent of "You've come a long way, baby!" The times were definitely changing.

Five

My Journey Onward

One weekend I drove to Wilbur Hot Springs, one of my favorite get-away places neatly tucked away in the mountains near Clear Lake. A former Native American healing spot, the popular Hot Springs was well known for its invigorating mineral waters and its warm, congenial, spiritual atmosphere.

As I walked up the dirt road from the parking lot to the resort, I met two men who had also just arrived. I was surprised to discover that one of them, Shawn, was living in Sacramento with a woman named Kelly, with whom I had gone to high school in Connecticut. Her father had been the salty, gravel-voiced dispatcher at Teddy's Taxi where I had worked as a cab driver before coming to California.

Good old Harry. It was his gruff but lovable voice over our two-way radios that used to ask us our location, direct us around town, and then tell us to "Reeee-turn" after dropping off our fares. I remembered Harry on the platform of the Westport Railroad Station, his strikingly haggard and gaunt workingman presence in the midst of the well-dressed Westport commuters—how he piled them one by one into our cabs and sent us out into the night.

That hard-working, gray-haired taxi maestro had been the rock of my life as I fought to stay sane in a hometown that didn't work for me anymore. I would never forget his stoic, impenetrable gaze and the unspoken emotion I felt as I bade him farewell on my last day of work. His raspy but affectionate "Take care" rang in my ears as I traveled across the country. Driving through the Badlands, I wouldn't have been surprised at all if Harry's voice had broken in over my radio with "Eighty-two, where are you, Warren?" And I would say, "South Dakota, Harry—long ways from home, Harry. Kinda scared, Harry."

"Reeee-turn, Eighty-two," he would say.

"Can't, Harry," I would tell him. "Gotta find myself, Harry. Over."

But in that remote northern California Hot Springs, it clearly wasn't over as I indirectly crossed paths with my old boss. What a coincidence. Little did I realize that the "chance" encounter with Shawn was just the beginning of a synchronistic weekend that would end up sending me to Sacramento, even to Shawn and Kelly's house.

We continued our conversation as we soaked in the soothing warm mineral waters at Wilbur. Shawn filled me in on all the years since I had last seen Kelly. She was now a teacher in Sacramento. And Harry was retired from the taxi business. I couldn't imagine the Westport Railroad Station without him.

Shawn and his friend and I ended up talking some more in the living room of the huge old resort. There was an air of receptivity and acceptance at Wilbur that made it easy for people to get together and talk. It was like a spiritual coffeehouse where people could enter into easy conversation and share deeply what was happening in their lives.

I was intrigued by the pieces of conversation that floated by— sometimes in the large old living room, but especially in the mineral baths themselves. As guests huddled in the warm waters, there was even more openness, for much of the conversation centered on spiritual topics. People talked animatedly about spiritual teachers, recent workshops, and personal growth.

Many guests were getting a massage, so there was quite a bit of talk in the waters about the subject—the therapeutic benefits of massage, the different kinds of bodywork, and places where you could take classes and get certified. In at least three separate conversations, the name of the Sacramento Holistic Health Institute came up. I heard how spiritual it was, what good teachers they had, and in particular what an excellent certification program they had for therapeutic massage. Why was I being surrounded by talk about that particular place? Was somebody trying to tell me something?

Having watched the relaxed, contented people streaming back from their sessions with the Wilbur masseuse, and because of all the discussion about massage and massage schools, I decided to join the crowd. I made an appointment.

As I sat waiting for my massage, I thought about how satisfying it must be to work as a massage therapist. In social work I seldom saw the results of my work with clients, but in massage it seemed that it would be just the opposite.

When my appointment time came, I was a little awkward because I had never had a formal massage before, but the masseuse was friendly and quickly put me at ease. Soon her expert hands were working miracles on my tired muscles. When she finally finished, I thought I was in heaven. I hadn't known it was possible to feel that good. I quickly understood why everyone had been coming back to the mineral waters looking so relaxed.

I was surprised, however, when the masseuse asked me if I would mind working on her. She said she was tight from working on so many people. I told her that I had no idea what to do, but I would be glad to give it a try. She said she'd talk me through it. Twenty minutes later, she said she was feeling much better and that I had a gift for massage. I was pleased. She even suggested that I consider getting trained and certified. And I wasn't surprised when she recommended the Sacramento Holistic Health Institute. The entire weekend from start to finish was pointing me toward that place. Was this yet another "divine" leading? I was almost getting used to them.

Back at work the next week, I learned that the Sacramento Holistic Health Institute was about to begin a new certification class. I made the three-and-a-half-hour round trip to Sacramento the next day to check out the program. The class met on Friday nights and all day Saturday and Sunday for several months. I would have to stay in Sacramento every weekend, but I was ready to do anything to get certified.

I was hoping to find some inexpensive housing in Sacramento and told a friend at work about my situation. He said that he had an old girlfriend who lived in Sacramento and he would contact her. Maybe she would have some ideas. He came back into my office later, rolling his eyes and shaking his head in disbelief.

"Warren, I just talked with her. She said she goes to Sonoma every weekend to stay with her boyfriend and that you are welcome to stay in her apartment." Peering out at me from behind his glasses with a wide-eyed "How in the world do you do it?" look, my friend added, "She also told me that she lives within walking distance of the Sacramento Holistic Health Institute." Still shaking his head, he returned to his office. He would never be able to figure me out.

2

So the Sacramento Holistic Health Institute massage certification program was the next stop on my spiritual journey. The Institute itself was primarily devoted to metaphysical study. The program had courses in yoga, meditation, Tai Chi, and rebirthing, as well as certification programs for holistic health practitioners and, of course, massage therapists. The term "holistic health" described an organized health care system that stressed wellness rather than sickness and emphasized the unity of body, mind, and spirit. The emerging holistic health field was attempting to help people take responsibility for their physical, mental, and spiritual well being. The use of daily exercises, sound nutrition, and spiritual practice was part of the lifestyle.

The spiritual underpinnings of the Sacramento Holistic Health Institute were completely in tune with my metaphysical beliefs. It didn't matter if you were a Native American healer or a Tibetan monk—there was lots of common ground.

Our instructors were a young couple who were into metaphysical spirituality, concentrating especially in the area of rebirthing. In their private practice they helped people relax back to their birth or to the early stages of their childhood, where traumas and other emotional blocks could be re-experienced and worked through. They were professional, and their enthusiastic acceptance of alternative spiritual principles transformed what could have been a rote class on massage techniques into a class on spiritual healing.

My classmates came from widely varying backgrounds, but we all seemed to share the basic desire to be channels of love, light, and healing. We wanted to learn to "open ourselves up" so that the healing energy of the universe could flow through us and into our clients.

The days of instruction were long, but much of the time I was on a massage table with someone practicing on me. That was one of the great benefits of the class. We were always working on each other as we perfected our techniques.

3

One day, a friend in the class loaned me a book called *Love Is Letting Go of Fear,* by Gerald Jampolsky. The book had an instant and profound effect upon me.

Dr. Jampolsky's book was consistent with my other metaphysical teachings. He emphasized that only as I cleared up my old negative thought system would I start to experience love and inner peace. Only as I learned to let go of fear would I stop experiencing the attacks that I perceived as coming from the world but which were actually a result of my own negative thoughts.

We were all searching for a better way, and for Jampolsky a better way had been a three-volume set of books called *A Course in Miracles. Love Is Letting Go of Fear* was basically Jampolsky's resounding recommendation and personal testimonial to the effectiveness of *A Course in Miracles* as a form of spiritual psychotherapy.

He made it clear that A Course in Miracles had totally changed his life, and he made numerous references to the Course even before he began the first chapter. He was obviously convinced, and that convinced me. His enthusiastic endorsement of *A Course in Miracles* sent me to the nearest bookstore to buy the set.

When I walked into a downtown Sacramento bookstore, I was delighted to find "The Course" immediately. But as I flipped through the three-volume set of blue hardcover books I was taken aback by its use of Christian terminology. Words such as *salvation, atonement, Holy Spirit,* and *Son of God* seemed to predominate, and I was confused. Jampolsky had given no hint that the Course was Christian in nature. But as I continued to look through the books it seemed that the Course was really an attempt to re-explain the Bible and its teachings. I began to see that it was actually a radically modern look at what the Bible was really saying, in contrast to the incorrect teachings that were being taught in churches. I could see that the Course was trying to shed new light on a misunderstood subject. Nevertheless, I still found myself struggling with the explicitly Christian vocabulary. I would never have bought the Course on my own, but because Jampolsky's little book was based on the Course I figured it had to be good.

Wanting another opinion, though, I finally sidestepped over to a clerk and asked him, "Do you know anything about *A Course in Miracles?*"

He looked at me thoughtfully for a moment, and then with the most genuine smile he answered, "*A Course in Miracles* is *the* most profound spiritual experience I have ever had. I have been using it for about sixteen months, and it has totally changed my life."

Jampolsky couldn't have said it better. I bought the books. I would just have to learn to get used to the Christian terminology.

4

In June of 1981, I was officially certified as a massage practitioner by the Sacramento Holistic Health Institute. With my trusty portable massage table, I began working on friends and coworkers in my spare time. I even took my table into the board and care homes where I did my social work and started giving massages to my developmentally disabled clients. Sometimes I had to smile when they lined up with their shirts off, waiting for their turn. I also talked about my new spiritual ideas and practices. I soon had them meditating, visualizing, Sufi dancing, and even repeating affirmations. We were a wild bunch, but they liked me and trusted me.

So my new spiritual philosophy was already working through me and starting to bear fruit in the care homes of northern California. It seemed only natural to incorporate what I was learning into my work. I was enthusiastic, and no one seemed to mind. One of the highlights of my week was Sufi dancing at lunch hour with the developmentally disabled clients, at a sheltered workshop in a nearby town. We sang and chanted and danced as we celebrated a cross-section of religions, including Native American, Jewish, Buddhist, and Islamic traditions.

5

Meanwhile, Joy and I had stayed in touch. I often stopped by her house, and we talked for hours. There was a familiarity between us that almost defied description. We felt extremely comfortable with each other, and we could talk about almost anything with ease. There was a mutual respect based on our understanding the seriousness of the other's spiritual search.

Late one summer afternoon several weeks after I finished massage school, I took Joy for a canoe ride in a beautiful wooded, lagoon-like area near the Sacramento River. It was the closestthing we'd ever had to a date, and I was a little nervous because we weren't in our usual cafe, street corner, or living room setting. I remember being reflective and looking forward to having a good talk with the woman who had become my best friend.

As we pushed out into the water, we realized that we were all alone except for the heron wading across the way. It was quiet and still and reminded me of the South on soft summer afternoons. There was a richness in the air and a hint of simpler times. I felt close to Joy and cared for by her.

My relationship with her had continued to grow in the past six months, and as we continued to walk parallel paths, we always seemed to understand what the other was going through. The friendship was most unusual. I had never met anyone like Joy. A desire to know the truth emanated from her essence and maybe from mine, too. We recognized that spiritual thirst in each other and nurtured it.

I paddled out into the middle of the water. After catching up on all of our latest doings, we sat quietly for a while, not saying a word. With Joy, silence was okay. I didn't feel my usual need to talk or perform. She made me feel relaxed and at peace.

I thought about Joy's unique and special qualities. Looking into her eyes, I finally broke the several-minute silence. "Joy, whoever marries you will really be blessed," I said sincerely and from the bottom of my heart. She was a soft, sweet, gentle soul. She was not looking for worldly success or popularity. She just wanted to know God. How incredibly refreshing in this crazy old world! And although she meditated to contact the "God within," she also prayed to an external aspect of God that was mysteriously "out there," too.

She wanted to get closer to the outside God. She wanted to bridge the gap somehow. And she had a relationship with this God that I could sense and see. It was real and honest, and it moved me. It was strange, but sometimes being with Joy made me feel closer to whatever or whomever God was—within or without.

Joy was now looking at me and smiling. "You, too, Warren. Whoever marries you will be very blessed."

I squirmed uncomfortably, not at her compliment but at the thought of that kind of personal commitment. Marriage seemed unlikely for a guy like me. But what she said was sweet, and it made me feel good because I knew she meant it.

After the canoe ride we had a leisurely dinner at a little Mexican restaurant, and then we went on to another place for some apple pie. It had been a wonderful day. The intimacy had been unexpressed, but we both could feel it.

Several days later, Joy called me and told me in an unusually warm and affectionate way that she had enjoyed our canoe ride and dinner. She said she really liked "my energy." But there was something about the way she said it that scared me. And much later she told me that it had scared her, too. In fact, the intimation of intimacy frightened us both so much that it was almost an entire month before we spoke again, and when we did we quickly retreated into our usual friendship. Under the surface something was changing, however, and there was little either of us could do to escape it.

Six

The Mesmeric Meditation

In this transition time between what had been and what would be, I found that in my meditations and quiet times I was getting nostalgic about the "good old days" with Rajneesh and his sannyasins. The more I thought back to that wild and wonderful energy, the more I started second-guessing my decision to leave it. What had caused me to move away from it I still didn't know. I had done the only reasonable thing at the time—move on to other spiritual pursuits—but now I was wondering if maybe I should try to reconnect.

One Friday afternoon as I drove to a friend's place in the San Francisco Bay Area, I had plenty of time to think as I wound my way through the rural northern California countryside. I drove past the orchards and rice fields and thought of my rise and fall with Rajneesh—how my wacky, wonderful Technicolor movie had suddenly changed to black and white. What had happened? Was it God's timing, or had I chickened out?

As I finally worked my way through the streets of Berkeley, I decided that the only way to resolve my dilemma about Rajneesh would be to drive over to the Berkeley Rajneesh Center. As I walked in the door of the Center, I immediately saw a sannyasin I had met at Harbin earlier in the year. He ran over and gave me a big hug. When I told him that I had spontaneously decided to drop by the Center to see what was going on, he looked at me in amazement and said, "My friend, you have obviously been divinely led. Teertha is here for the weekend, and he is giving a special two-day workshop that starts tomorrow!"

My whole being went numb. I could hardly believe it. Teertha, Bhagwan's second in command, the master of the encounter groups in India—here in Berkeley? It was almost too much to comprehend. Without even trying, I had just walked back into the Rajneesh electric zone.

My friend laughed, knowing I had never expected that kind of news. He told me that the workshop was $100 and they were only taking cash. When I said that cash would be a problem, a $100 bill was suddenly draped over the shoulder of the person standing next to me. I did a double take as I recognized Yatri, a sannyasin whom I had met through Veena and Dharmananda. He was there for the workshop with Teertha. With a big smile on his face, he told me to take the $100 bill and pay him back later. I thanked him, took the money, and immediately signed up for the workshop. I wondered if I was about to return to everything I thought I had left behind. I was back with Rajneesh, at least for the weekend.

2

The next morning, I sat in the Berkeley meditation hall with about one hundred other people. There was a keen sense of anticipation as we all stretched and meditated and did deep breathing while we awaited Teertha and his sannyasin entourage. When the retinue arrived, the room became charged with energy, and I was at once struck by Teertha's dynamic and charismatic presence. He was wearing a long robe, and he glided into the room with effortless grace. He assumed a cross-legged position in front of us. The ten or fifteen sannyasins with him sat in an orderly group behind him, heightening the drama of his impressive entrance.

Teertha said nothing for several minutes as he stared out into the faces of the predominantly orange crowd. His head moved methodically up and down as his eyes seemed to lock in and make contact with each of us. It was as if he was checking in and out of our energy fields. I suddenly felt transparent and vulnerable. There was an undefined spiritual presence about him that was unsettling and somewhat disturbing. Yet I knew that his confrontational style was probably just another Rajneesh device to help me grow.

After Teertha led a meditation and did a number of individual encounters and interactions with various people, the morning was quickly gone. During the lunch break I ate with a young couple who lived in my area. I recognized the woman from a workshop I had attended earlier in the year.

After lunch I still felt some uneasiness about the workshop, but I was ready to dive into the afternoon session. After a few more individual encounters with people, Teertha announced that we were going to do a guided exercise. He told us to start walking around the room. We were to feel the energy of those walking around us and gravitate toward the person we seemed to have the most energy for. Opposite sex. Same sex. It didn't matter. He told us to take our time and to feel it out. As he talked, his voice sounded ethereal and sing-songy.

A bit apprehensive, I was glad when the woman I had just eaten lunch with became my partner. She also seemed relieved to be with someone she knew. We stood side by side waiting for whatever would come next.

Teertha, seeing that everyone had paired up, told us to express the energy we were feeling for our partner in any way we wanted—with a dance, a smile, a kiss, a hug—whatever. I gave my partner a hug, and she hugged me back.

Teertha's voice seemed to stretch into a new tonal scale, becoming even more melodious and hypnotic as he urged us to a more intense expression of the energy we were feeling for the person we were with. Awkwardly, I hugged my partner again, but this time I also gave her a little kiss on the cheek.

Teertha continued in full form and told us to drop all preconceived notions of who we were or what seemed to be right or wrong. With great persuasiveness he tried to convince us to let go of all fears, all blocks and hang-ups. We should completely let go of anything that would keep us from the fullest expression of the energy we were feeling. It was absolutely essential that we go with our energy.

By that point, I wasn't sure what Teertha was doing, but the almost mesmeric tone of his voice was making me uneasy. The room was starting to heat up, and I could sense that some people were really getting into the exercise. I stood with my partner not knowing what to do. She was as reluctant as I to go along with the exercise.

Teertha then moved into full stride, cajoling, beseeching, almost taunting us with his smooth hypnotic coercion. "Drop all notions of who you are or who the other is. Just be. Let go. Express the feelings. Don't be afraid. Don't hold back."

My body was starting to tremble with resistance because I was not convinced, and I was not comfortable with what was happening in the room. Although I was familiar with the liberality of personal expression in the Rajneesh movement, this was far beyond anything I had ever imagined.

There was a heavy, hungry aura of sexuality hovering over the meditation hall. It didn't feel spiritual, and it didn't feel right. In fact, it seemed dark. My friend and I continued to hold back. Neither of us could pretend to go on with the so-called exercise. We just waited it out.

When it was finally over, I wondered if Teertha's words had put some of the people in the room into a trance. A number of them were still putting on their clothes. A master mesmerizer had played sex in the name of spirituality to the hilt.

I understood at once that spirituality could take a sudden twisted turn at any moment. I realized that my separation from Rajneesh had been the right move. By virtue of Teertha's proximity to Rajneesh I could no longer trust Rajneesh as I had. I would not forget my sannyasin friends and the truths that I had been taught by Rajneesh, but it was now clear that my days with Rajneesh were over.

I said so long to my friend, thankful that she had been my partner. I doubted she or her boyfriend would be back for the second day of the workshop either.

As I left the meditation hall and the Center, I was still shaking my head. I didn't know it, but I had been mercifully spared reinvolvement in a movement that would continue to gather momentum, with Rajneesh moving his ashram from India to Oregon—ultimately exploding with guns and embezzlement and threats of murder. I was grateful to have been shown some of the darkness that was behind the "light" of Rajneesh.

Seven

My Friend the Channeler

During the fall of 1981, I continued trying to integrate everything I had been learning into my life. I meditated, visited the local psychic, used my massage skills as much as possible, and started studying *A Course in Miracles*. I was trying to become a more positive person as I learned that most of my problems came from my own wrong perceptions. As the year came to a close, I could feel an old part of myself dying. I was being spiritually born into my ever-expanding metaphysical belief system.

In February 1982, my friend Taylor and I were asked by our employer to transport a developmentally disabled client from a state hospital to a residential care home near Mount Shasta. Taylor and I decided to drive down to Napa Valley the day before so we could get a good start the next day. We arrived in the nearby town of Calistoga in the early afternoon and checked into Nance's Hot Springs Motel. While Taylor went in to Napa on some work-related business, I stayed at Nance's to relax.

Somewhat stressed from work, I was glad to have time to unwind. I sat in the mineral waters for an hour or so before taking one of their famous volcanic mud baths and getting a half-hour massage. Then I floated back into the locker room. I felt renewed.

After taking a shower and getting dressed, I leaned down to tie my shoe just as the man next to me leaned down to tie his. Aware of our simultaneous shoe-tying, we introduced ourselves. As we started to talk, we quickly realized that we had a lot in common. Jeremy was a young psychologist. I was a social worker. He was deeply involved in his own personal and spiritual growth, and so was I. He, too, was disenchanted and disillusioned by traditional forms of religion and psychology.

71

Jeremy went on to tell me that he was working with an interesting and most unusual man who lived in a neighboring town. When he told me the man had clairvoyant abilities, I could feel him studying me and waiting to see my reaction. When I told him about Bonnie and Carolyn and that I was okay with psychics, he relaxed and opened up.

He told me that he thought Sam, his clairvoyant friend, was on the cutting edge of a new spiritual phenomenon. He had been able to tap into the universal consciousness of humankind. Sam was a channeler, and he was channeling something that called itself "the Source" of the universe. The Source, or collective consciousness, spoke through Sam in a most remarkable and authoritative way.

When I told Jeremy that my only familiarity with channeling was from Jane Roberts' "Seth" books, he quickly explained that Sam was not channeling a spiritual entity as Roberts had, but rather he was channeling a collective consciousness. He said that the Source even used the pronoun "we" when speaking through him. Jeremy also made it clear that Sam did not go into a trance state the way most channelers did. He was active and alert, but he remained in the background as the Source spoke through him. He was as much of an observer as anyone else in the room. He could hear what the Source was saying and could even break in with his own personality if he had to. It was as if Sam the man stepped back so that the Source could come through.

Thoroughly intrigued, I suggested that we continue our conversation in my room. Once we were settled and comfortable, Jeremy's countenance lit up as he described how Sam, an unlikely Napa Valley farmer, had gone from meditation to channeling in almost no time flat. Jeremy was both amazed and mystified by this middle-aged family man who was so seemingly ordinary in his appearance and everyday life but so extraordinary in his ability to channel the Source.

My new friend went on to tell me that he and Sam had met at an Inner Light Consciousness (ILC) workshop put on by the noted Virginia Beach channeler, healer, and metaphysical authority Paul Solomon. Solomon had explained to everyone that he was channeling the Source and that it was an expression of universal truth. His ILC workshops were his way of communicating to those interested the specific tools and techniques that would enable each student or seeker to attain their own personal relationship with the Source. One of the first things he taught was how to develop a positive, loving relationship with yourself.

Jeremy related that Sam took down all that Solomon said and started incorporating everything he had learned into his daily life. For days on end Sam worked with the Solomon material. He listened to his tapes, did his meditations, and kept the recommended comprehensive spiritual journal. In the journal he recorded dreams, wrote "Dear Master" (higher self) letters, and did the other various journal entries that helped him with his spiritual problem solving. Sam became almost fanatical in his involvement with the Solomon material.

And then one day in the midst of all this zealous discipline and dedication, an audible inner voice punched through into Sam's consciousness and started talking to him and through him. To Sam's utter and absolute delight, the voice announced itself as the famous Source. He was convinced it was the universal Source that spoke through Solomon, but, of course, universal truth has to work through the filter of each individual's beliefs and experiences. Sam did not pretend to be as "clear" as Solomon or other enlightened or nearly enlightened men. But he was channeling the Source.

Jeremy said that when Sam told him he was channeling the Source, he was totally blown away. Sam seemed such an unlikely vehicle for this higher consciousness. But what did he know? What did anybody know? Life was always full of surprises. Jeremy figured that if Sam could tap into the Source, maybe he could, too.

Perhaps it was really available to anyone who was willing to seek it out. So Jeremy decided to move up to the Napa Valley to study and work with his friend who had become an oracle overnight. Jeremy was determined to learn as much as he could from Sam's Source so that he could apply what he learned to his own spiritual life. Maybe someday he, too, could channel the Source.

So Jeremy had packed up his things and left his L.A. life behind. Like sannyasins and so many others I had met on the spiritual path, there was little he wouldn't do in his search for truth. Jeremy and I were alike. If someone told us that truth was in Nebraska, we would be there in the morning. There was an undefinable urgency to our search. It was an insatiable desire to cut through all the superficiality and falsity we felt and to get down to what was real.

As I listened to Jeremy, I saw that he was much like myself in other ways, too. He was excited by the search for spiritual truth, and the desire of his heart was to be a more loving and spiritual person and to help others. He wanted to point people toward peace, healing, and God.

Jeremy looked at me and seemed to echo my thoughts. "Warren, there is so much we need to do to get ourselves together. Spiritual growth is mandatory for our planet and our people. We have to get past our day-to-day hang-ups with each other. We have to learn how to forgive—and how to truly love—and spiritually evolve."

Jeremy spent another hour or so telling me everything he had been learning from the Source. He talked about its emphasis on good diet and cleansing the body through periodic fasting, its enthusiastic endorsement of A *Course in Miracles*, and answers that he and Sam had received to questions they had asked about a wide range of issues, including cures for cancer.

Jeremy and I had been talking animatedly for several hours and by now were spiritually soaring. We seemed to validate and energize each other. I was convinced that Jeremy and I had not met by chance and that both he and Sam would become an important part of my continued growth. We decided that I would go to Sam's place in several weeks to meet him. Jeremy gave me the address and phone number. It had been quite an afternoon.

2

When Taylor and I got home, I told Joy everything that had happened. As I described Jeremy and what he had told me about Sam, Joy was curious. She was familiar with the concept of channeling but had never actually met anyone who was doing it. I told her I would give her a full report after I saw them.

Several weeks later, I stopped by Joy's house to say good-bye before I set out for my visit with Sam and Jeremy. Sitting on her front porch, we talked about my trip and what might happen. I told her that I thought it was going to be one of the most important things I would ever do in my life. I could sense that I was moving into a much more accelerated phase of my spiritual growth. She was excited for me. She was perhaps the only person who knew how serious I was about my spiritual life. She understood because she felt the same way.

I drove to Nance's Hot Springs where I would again spend the night before going over to see Sam and Jeremy the next morning. As I sat in the warmth of Nance's soothing mineral waters, I thought about my meeting with Sam and Jeremy and wondered how it would go. I was excited.

That night in my sleep, the face of a man I had never seen before came to me in a dream, hovering before me and staring at me for a moment or two before floating away. It was most unusual, and I could not remember anything quite like it ever happening before. The presence almost seemed real.

When I arrived at Sam's house the next morning and he came to the door, I was a little unnerved to find myself shaking hands with the man from my dream. There was no mistaking his unusual features. I had read about people having precognitive dreams, but this was a first for me. I chose to see it as a sign that what I was doing was meant to be.

Sam was very much as Jeremy had described him. A nonsense working man with a strikingly ordinary physical appearance, he had a gravelly, guttural voice and spoke in a monotone. He punctuated his sentences with the expression "whatever" or "whatever is happening."

It was agreed that before Sam did any channeling for me I would spend time with Jeremy getting a general overview of their work and discussing what we would be doing during the next several days. He would also give me some ideas on how to get in touch with what they called my "higher self," as well as give me handouts and other information.

The first hour or so, Jeremy talked about the differences between the lower, middle, and higher selves. Using a process he called "voice dialogue," he helped me to understand the tension between the three parts of myself. Each self had its own characteristic way of dealing with situations. He showed me ways to work with my subconscious mind and also how to make contact with my higher self more effectively. He also described Sam's Source in detail. The two of them had done readings on everything from past lives to future world events. The Source was tuned into everyone and everything and would offer answers or advice on any question or problem.

Jeremy went on to discuss a number of other spiritual topics, talking about Edgar Cayce, Carl Jung, the Hawaiian Kahunas, *A Course in Miracles*, and Paul Solomon. Jeremy was an interesting and disciplined teacher, and I respected him already.

After two hours or so, Sam came into the room. He asked me if I was ready for my reading, and I said yes. He closed his eyes for a couple of moments, and when he opened them again he said the Source was ready. I could ask whatever questions I wanted.

In the next two hours I asked a number of questions about my job, personal relationships, health problems, specific hangups, and spiritual direction. The answers were usually specific and accurate in regard to things that were verifiable, and plausible in those areas that were more speculative and subjective. I was impressed.

At one point in the reading, Jeremy asked me if I wanted to know what soul level I was on, so I asked. The Source, speaking through Sam, said, "We would say that you are a level four. You are an advanced soul, having learned many important lessons in past lives. You have a ways to go yet but are now in a position to make rapid soul growth. The coming days are days of opportunity for those who wish to move quickly and grow beyond old habits and behaviors and programming. You have the potential to be an effective teacher of spiritual principles."

Hearing that I was an advanced soul with the potential to be a spiritual teacher was encouraging. Most of what the Source told me in our readings that first day was optimistic and uplifting.

The Source said that many of the people in my life were souls whom I had been close to in other lives and that we were continuing to work through things in this life. What was most important was complete forgiveness and unconditional love.

Because the Source could see into my body and knew my body's chemistry, it told me in a "body reading" that I had a high level of toxicity in my system and an extended Spirulina and juice fast was highly recommended. They told me that I could call Sam during my fast and do "spot readings" on my progress. The Source would let me know when my body was cleaned out and I could end the fast.

As I sat with Sam and Jeremy, I marveled at how the universe had brought us together and was now communicating so effectively to me through this most unusual man. I was grateful for the spiritual help I was receiving. Laughing, Sam told me I was getting a three-day "crash course on the universe." I knew he was right.

One afternoon during my visit, Jeremy and Sam told me they needed to communicate some serious concerns to me. I sat down and braced myself for whatever was so important.

Jeremy, loosely quoting Edgar Cayce and backing his statement with readings from Sam's Source, told me that the coming years were going to be spiritually spectacular but also difficult, even cataclysmic, for planet Earth.

"We have lived so long in spiritual ignorance," Jeremy explained, "that mankind is in a very negative space. Our personal lives and the life of the planet itself have been tainted and spoiled and defiled by centuries of misuse and abuse."

Both men related that in the not-so-distant future there would be a series of what they called "earth changes," as predicted by Cayce, the Source, and many other psychics around the world. As humanity shifted from its obsolete belief systems toward a new spiritual awareness, the earth would need to cleanse itself from the years of accumulated negativity. Earthquakes and other extreme conditions would manifest during this period of earth changes.

Both men stressed that only those people who were willing to realign themselves with what was true and real would survive the shifts that would occur. In the shift in consciousness that would accompany the earth changes, those souls who could not stand the heat of spiritual transformation and who persisted in selfish, outmoded belief systems would drown in the tide of the times.

Sam and Jeremy made it clear that the coming earth changes and accompanying spiritual transformation were both desirable and necessary. Only after the mandatory cleansing would there be peace and true spiritual brotherhood on our planet. The gravity of their message was sobering, but I accepted their words. I knew we all had to get serious about our spiritual lives and that as we worked toward a lasting oneness and peace on the planet some would always fight the change and choose to live in the darkness of their ignorance. I wondered how much time we had left. It might be closer than I thought. I wasn't sure the Source would answer that one, but I really didn't want to know anyway. The whole subject made me quite solemn.

I spent three days with Sam and Jeremy getting my "crash course on the universe." In many ways it reinforced things I already believed, while adding many new bits and pieces to my emerging belief system.

I did a lot of Source readings while there, and Sam, Jeremy, and the Source encouraged me to continue my meditation with a special Solomon meditation. I was also advised to keep a comprehensive spiritual journal, along the lines of the one devised by Solomon. I was told to begin writing "Dear Master" letters and to depend more and more on my own inner guidance. I was also instructed to dig ever deeper into A Course in Miracles, as well as study the various tapes and other Solomon material they gave me.

I knew I would be staying in close contact with Sam and Jeremy and that I would want to continue using Sam's Source until I could more completely trust my inner guidance from my higher self. I was committed to spiritual growth and wanted to be correct in whatever I did in life—whether it was as a social worker or as a spiritual teacher.

At the end of our time together, I thanked Sam and Jeremy for their time and energy. I was loaded down with books, tapes, and handouts and was now well into the next phase of my personal spiritual transformation. I was surprised that Sam charged me so reasonably for his time and materials. But he and Jeremy genuinely seemed to like me. They believed that the universe was preparing me for work similar to theirs. Already they felt like friends and partners in a joint spiritual venture.

It was a beautiful sunny day as I drove back through the orchards and rice fields of northern California. I looked east to the mountains and felt a surge of gratitude for what was happening in my life.

As I neared home, I realized I was gaining a new personal and spiritual confidence. After all these years, I was finally starting to understand who I was and what life was all about. And while I continued to reprogram my subconscious mind with positive affirmations, I would work to develop a better relationship with my higher self.

On paper it seemed simple. We were already a perfect part of God, but there were still clouds of illusion in the way. That was what spiritual discipline was all about—trying to dissolve those clouds through the practice of truth and get back to the simplicity of love.

As I pulled into my driveway, I knew that my visit with Sam and Jeremy had already changed my life. I felt a new excitement and urgency. It was important that I get as clear as possible, as quickly as possible. If I was going to teach these spiritual principles someday, I would have to get my act together in a hurry. A lot would be coming down, with the earth changes and all. I wanted to do everything I could to help prepare people for the coming times. One of the things I knew I wanted to do was have Sam and Jeremy come to my house to talk to my friends. The least I could do under the circumstances was to help teach what I was trying to learn.

Eight

Course in Miracles Connection

It wasn't long before we set the date for Sam and Jeremy to visit, and on the appointed night friends and co-workers gathered at my house. They were eager to meet the channeler I had been talking about.

As everyone began to gather, the phone rang. It was Jeremy. He said that he and Sam had just run out of gas. They were stranded south of town some fifteen miles away. I stood with the phone in my hand, shaking my head in disbelief. The channeler who was privy to the secrets of the universe had run out of gas. I couldn't believe it. The workshop was scheduled to start in thirty minutes. What could I do except try to be understanding and tell Jeremy that I would pick up some gas and be right over?

Trying to appear upbeat and anything but embarrassed, I told everyone what had happened and that I'd be right back. Not quite escaping out the front door, I was stopped by a friend from Sacramento who voiced my own thoughts. "How together is your friend? This guy is a crack psychic and he runs out of gas?"

There was muffled laughter from the others, and I tried to downplay my discomfort by saying something about all of us being human. But I was definitely unnerved. How could they? Finally, seeing the situation as a lesson in learning to be joyful in the midst of trying circumstances, I let my feelings go.

After I picked up some gas and finally pulled up next to Sam's motor home on the side of the highway, I was surprised to find him as nonchalant as ever. His response to the situation was, "Whatever is happening."

Jeremy was more apologetic as he told me that Sam had done a reading on the gas situation and had been told by the Source that they would run out of gas. Sam had chosen to override the Source's warning by gambling that they could make it. Jeremy and I agreed that Sam's lesson for the day was that he might be channeling the truth of the universe, but he still had to apply it to his life to make it work.

Finally, we all pulled into my house almost an hour late for the scheduled workshop. I relaxed when people were forgiving, and after some basic introductions we formed a big circle in the living room and began the program.

Jeremy kicked things off by giving a rundown of metaphysical principles. He stressed the importance of taking responsibility for our thought lives. We choose what we think and feel, he said, and in effect we create our own reality. He talked about our need to overcome our negative subconscious programs. And he went into considerable detail on the necessity of retraining our minds through positive affirmations so that we could receive good inner guidance from our higher self. His talk was instructive, and people seemed interested.

At that point, Sam took over and described his experiences with channeling. It had taken much discipline and spiritual work to clear the inner way so the Source could speak through him. Then, for more than two hours Sam channeled the Source and answered questions from the group on almost every imaginable subject. It was a lively exchange as the Source demonstrated an often shockingly accurate depth of knowledge about people's personal lives. It told them about current and upcoming relationships, childhood dynamics, vocational trends, health issues, and even past lives. The evening went well, and a number of people scheduled private readings with Sam. He had agreed to stay at my house for just that purpose.

For the next two days, people streamed in and out of my house to talk with Sam and the Source. It was fun to be a part of my friends' growth process by providing them the opportunity to work with a channeler. I knew I was at the forefront of something of tremendous spiritual significance.

After my friends had gotten their readings, Sam volunteered to do one for me as thanks for setting everything up. I asked a number of questions on a variety of subjects, but perhaps most interesting was the Source's description of a past life I'd had in frontier America.

I was told that I had traveled around to various outposts and other sparsely settled areas to encourage people and give them counsel. I had gone wherever I was needed. The Source said that I had brought the gifts of that life to my present job as a social worker. My job with Traveler's Aid on the streets of San Francisco and my work as an itinerant social worker in rural northern California were direct expressions of that former life.

Then the Source went on to tell me that the freelance frontier counseling *then* and the street work and itinerant social work *now* were all part of a plan to prepare me for the spiritual work I was about to begin. My soul's purpose in this lifetime was to be a spiritual teacher. I had an important role to play, and I would be part of the spiritual awareness movement that would help the world get back on track. I had specifically volunteered for this role before even entering this present life.

After a most interesting three days, Sam and Jeremy headed back to the Napa Valley with the satisfaction of knowing they had sparked metaphysical interest among my friends and made a spiritual mark in my town.

Sam was not someone I would have ordinarily gone out of my way to meet, let alone become friends with, but the almost inexhaustible enthusiasm we shared for spiritual things helped us transcend our personality differences. We shared a higher purpose, and it was in that purpose that we bonded together.

In the following weeks I called Sam frequently. I got "spot readings" on a number of concerns, including the progress of my fast that the Source had recommended. The Source monitored the fast by giving me almost daily reports on my physical condition. In effect, the Source was my doctor.

It seemed strange that the Source could read me so completely. It was as if I was mentally, physically, and spiritually transparent. But I knew that Edgar Cayce had done the same thing—and with proven results. I had read that he had performed trance-channeled readings and helped hundreds of people with his supernatural counsel and many more with his published writings.

Edgar Cayce, Paul Solomon, and now Sam were demonstrating through their channeling that truth is available to us if we are willing to clear the way for the higher self and go within to seek its wisdom. We were finally starting to understand and believe the divine laws of the universe. Metaphysical spirituality was on the move.

Sam had suddenly put everything I was doing into fast forward. My spiritual life had a new acceleration and intensity that seemed to outdistance even my Rajneesh enthusiasm. I really was getting a crash course from the universe, and I could see that I was being prepared to be a spiritual teacher. Old mindsets were colliding with a new powerful, positive, spiritual reality, and it was exciting to be a part of the transformation.

So I continued my close contact with Sam, both on the phone and in person. The Source continued to help me find direction and to point me toward the experiences and relationships that were in my best interest.

2

On my next visit to the Napa Valley, I was shocked when Jeremy took me aside and told me that he was moving back to southern California. He said that he had become too dependent on Sam's Source and that he needed to start getting more of his own answers. He said it was time for him to develop a better relationship with the Source through his *own* higher self. I'll never forget his look when he told me not to confuse Sam the man with the Source that spoke through Sam. They were not the same, and I should be very careful to remember that.

I was sorry to see Jeremy leave my life so quickly, and I thanked him for everything he had done. We promised to stay in touch and believed that our paths would cross again.

Almost before I knew it, I was Sam's new protege, and I moved into Jeremy's position as chief student apprentice. Sam and I often traveled back and forth between each other's homes. He would do readings, share spiritual insights, give me books, and bring all sorts of interesting things to my attention. We did spot readings on our early morning runs or as we drove in his pickup truck. It was unique to have a channeler as a friend. And it was remarkable that he was always fully conscious when the Source spoke through him. Even Cayce and Solomon couldn't do that.

Though I was getting tremendous encouragement and support from Sam and the Source, I also knew that my friendship was important to him. He was a different kind of guy, and although he had a wife and two children he didn't have many friends. He appreciated my visits and phone calls. I suppose somehow I validated him as a person by choosing him as my friend and spiritual teacher.

I actually became quite fond of Sam. Other than Jeremy, I had never met another man who was so completely absorbed in spiritual things. We were an odd pair, but we wanted nothing less than a total transformation of body, mind, soul, and spirit.

3

In the spring of 1982, Sam's family and I went down to Monterey for a three-day workshop on healing put on by the Edgar Cayce organization (A.R.E.) at the beautiful oceanfront conference center of Asilomar.

Sam and I were both fascinated by the readings and teachings and supernatural healings that had been done through Cayce when he channeled. We were particularly interested in the workshop because we had been told that a number of high-powered metaphysical speakers would be on hand, including some of Cayce's top people from Virginia Beach.

However, we were greatly disappointed by what we perceived to be an air of spiritual indifference hanging over the program and characterizing the crowd in attendance. We were sadly reminded of churches we had attended where people came for social rather than spiritual reasons. Although there were a few good speakers and some nice people, all in all the predominant attitude was one of self-congratulation and spiritual complacency. We didn't want to be judgmental, but the weekend felt more like an Edgar Cayce Moose Lodge than a spiritual conference.

More than anything else at the conference, Sam and I enjoyed running in the mornings along the famous Seventeen Mile Drive. We rose early and jogged along the beach and did spot readings as we ran out past the million-dollar homes. It was a great way to start the day.

Perhaps the high point of the weekend for me was when I finally met the famous Frank Phillips. Throughout the conference I kept hearing his name. When I told people where I lived they invariably said, "Then you must know Frank Phillips. He lives in the town right next to you!"

I was told in glowing terms that this longtime A.R.E. member was a revered metaphysical teacher. Everyone seemed to love and respect him, and I was disappointed that he hadn't made it to the conference. Then, on the last day at lunch, the man sitting next to me said, "Oh, there's Frank Phillips and his wife!"

Instantly I was on my way over to him. I could see that he was a solid, gray-haired bear of a man, probably in his late sixties, with twinkly eyes and a wonderful, full-faced grin. I introduced myself and told him where I lived. We talked for a bit before he extended his providential invitation. "We're starting *A Course in Miracles* group at our house. Why don't you join us?"

I could hardly believe my ears. His invitation was like an answer to prayer. I had been reading the Course on my own, but I knew I needed to get involved in some kind of study group. So I welcomed Frank's invitation. At last, people to talk to about the Course and a qualified teacher to answer my questions!

I told Frank and his wife Trudy that I'd love to be in their group. Then, excusing myself, I went over to the table where Sam was sitting and told him about my meeting with them.

"Whatever is happening," was all he said.

On our way back to the Napa Valley after the conference and a side trip to Big Sur, we drove north on Highway 1. Looking out at the ocean, I thought about the Cayce conference and how it had been redeemed by my fortuitous meeting with Frank and his wife. As we worked our way along the curving coastal highway, I replayed Frank's enthusiastic invitation over and over in my mind. "We're starting *A Course in Miracles* group at our house. Why don't you join us?"

Nine

The Rolling Mystery School

As soon as I got home, I called Frank and Trudy, and the wheels were set in motion for the first meeting of our Course *in Miracles* group. On the appointed night I headed to their house. When I arrived, Frank and Trudy greeted me warmly and showed me into their expansive family room where we were meeting. Frank beamed as he made it a point to tell me that it was my interest which had finally gotten the group off the ground.

Only a few of us were there that first night, but in the coming weeks and months the group grew. Tuesday nights became a special night for all of us as we discussed and studied *A Course in Miracles*. For the next two years the Course group would be the focal point of my week and the Course itself a most important part of my life.

Frank was an excellent teacher. He was knowledgeable, patient, and full of enthusiasm. There was plenty of warmth and laughter as we studied the Course, and in time the group started to feel like family.

That first night, Frank described the origin of the Course. One day a respected New York City psychologist by the name of Helen Schucman heard an "inner voice" that told her, "This is *A Course in Miracles*. Please take notes." For more than seven years, that "inner voice," identifying itself as "Jesus," dictated the body of material that was eventually published as *A Course in Miracles*.

Frank gave us an overview of the Course, briefly outlining the three-volume 1,200-page work and explaining the differences between the Text, the Workbook, and the Teacher's Manual. He told us with obvious admiration that the Course was the most comprehensive spiritual work he had ever read. It crystallized the metaphysical teachings he had been studying for many years.

He told us that the Course had been sent to dispel the erroneous, fear-based notions which had been associated with the Bible's teachings. Frank said that the Course was a gift to help everyone understand what Jesus' teachings really meant. It explained that God is in everyone and everything and that we are all a part of God and God a part of us. We are one in spirit and in truth.

Frank told us that the Course's purpose was to deliver the real "good news." There is no sin, no devil, and no death. So there is no need for a Saviour to save us from imagined evils. As we become our own saviors and become part of the at-one-ment process, we undo our wrong thinking and start to share with others who we really are—sinless, guiltless Sons of God.

Frank emphasized that we are all "teachers of God" and that we all teach what we want to learn. And what we want to learn is love, because love is all there is. Everything else is illusion.

As Frank described the lesson book, he made it clear that by incorporating its truths into our lives we would be able to undo our wrong perceptions and see ourselves and others as we truly are. As he described our need for right thinking and clear perception, I looked randomly at some of the 365 daily lessons I would be affirming in the coming months:

Lesson 35	"My mind is part of God's. I am very holy."
Lesson 70	"My salvation comes from me."
Lesson 95	"I am one Self, united with my Creator."
Lesson 124	"Let me remember I am one with God."
Lesson 153	"In my defenselessness my safety lies."[1]

Later, Frank led us in a meditation, and then we broke for refreshments and lighter conversation. Frank's excitement about the Course was inspiring, and as I drove home I was filled with gratitude and thankfulness for Frank and Trudy, for the Course group, and to Jesus for sending us *A Course in Miracles.*

2

Sam and I often talked about *A Course in Miracles* but never in the depth of the Course group. He had already finished the Course, and although he was quick to acknowledge its importance in his life, we spent most of our time focused on other spiritual things—such as doing readings, listening to Paul Solomon's tapes, and discussing the latest books and workshops.

One day while I was visiting Sam, we drove over to Calistoga in the early afternoon to relax. While sitting in the mineral waters at one of the local health spas, we did some spot readings on a number of subjects, including my social life. I wasn't meeting anyone, and it was starting to bother me. I was feeling frustrated in my search for the perfect mate. Although Joy and I occasionally sensed that something else was going on between us, we really didn't seem to have *that* kind of relationship. So we continued to relate as friends. The Source had no immediate answers for me, except to remind me that I had jumped into relationships too quickly in the past and that I needed to be more patient.

Later, I joined Sam out on the patio as he read the latest newsletter from Paul Solomon's Virginia Beach Fellowship of the Inner Light. We could hardly contain ourselves when we saw the announcement: Teachers Training. Paul Solomon. Virginia Beach.

We didn't even flinch at the $2,500 tuition for the two-week workshop. We knew in our hearts that we were already on our way. It was one of those things that was meant to be, and, without even talking about it, we knew that the expenses of the trip would work themselves out. A spot reading from the Source confirmed everything we were feeling. It said we would make the trip to Virginia Beach and that it would play an important part in our continued spiritual growth.

Feeling great excitement, Sam and I jumped back into the mineral waters and started talking about Paul Solomon and his teachings. Solomon had apparently been a conservative preacher at one time, actually believing in the literal teachings of the Bible. Becoming disillusioned and oppressed by his faith, he started questioning his beliefs. Then one day in the middle of a session with a hypnotist, Solomon started speaking with an all-knowing voice that amazed the hypnotist with its range and breadth and depth of knowledge.

Soon Solomon was being put in a trance regularly and was doing readings on a variety of concerns and issues. The body of knowledge that came from those readings was consistent with a general metaphysical world view, and Solomon founded his Fellowship of the Inner Light on those channeled universal truths. Operating in the tradition of the ancient mystery schools, Solomon's teachings were highly eclectic and drew from a wide variety of spiritual disciplines. Now he was a well-known metaphysical teacher with Inner Light Consciousness (ILC) Centers scattered all over the world. From the Findhorn Community in Scotland to folks such as Sam and me, he had helped many people with his readings, teachings, and spiritual tools. Because of those teachings, Sam was now in touch with the Source, and his Source was now teaching me. Soon I, too, would play my part. Teachers Training. What could be more perfect?

I was fascinated by the fact that all of my new metaphysical understandings were almost magically intertwined and interconnected. A thread of consistency connected Bonnie, Rajneesh, Carolyn, the Sacramento Holistic Health Center, *A Course in Miracles*, Sam, the Source, Edgar Cayce, and Paul Solomon's Fellowship of the Inner Light. They were all different ways of approaching the universal oneness of God. *A Course in Miracles* said that as seekers we choose not the nature of the curriculum but the time we elect to spend learning it. Sam and I were willing to travel at the speed of light.

That afternoon as we drove back to Sam's house, we were flying high on our plans. We were already envisioning what could happen if we started our own northern California ILC Center after completing the Teachers Training. With Sam as a channeler and me as a counselor and massage therapist, we could see our emerging roles in the coming age of spiritual awareness.

Sam and I immediately sent in our registration forms. Because of my job and time constraints, I would later fly to Virginia Beach, and, in the meantime, Sam and his family would drive across the country in their motor home.

At my last *Course in Miracles* meeting before leaving for Virginia Beach, everyone wished me well. They all wanted a complete report when I got back.

Of course, I said good-bye to Joy. It didn't surprise her that I was taking off on yet another spiritual journey.

3

After arriving in Virginia Beach, I checked into my private room in the house of a local astrologer. I had gotten her name from the Edgar Cayce A.R.E. referral network. Sam, his wife, and their two boys had already arrived and were staying in their motor home. The California contingent was ready for the Teachers Training.

Solomon's Fellowship of the Inner Light was in a little neighborhood not far from downtown Virginia Beach. Solomon's staff was highly trained, and each of them had special expertise in the various topics that would be presented during the training—dreams, meditation, journal writing, spiritual problem solving, and learning to access the Source through the higher self.

Solomon would speak several times during the two-weeks' training, but the rest of the teaching would be done by his staff. The two weeks would culminate in each of us giving a presentation to the class that would be videotaped and critiqued by everyone else. At the end of the training, each one would have an individual conference with Solomon in which he would give us feedback on our performance and talk to us about where we were heading as spiritual teachers.

The group in attendance came from all over the United States and even from overseas. All of us were anxious to take advantage of the accelerated work Solomon was doing, largely based, of course, on his channeled understandings from the Source.

On the first evening, there was an air of anticipation as we waited for Paul Solomon to deliver his opening remarks and introductory lecture. At last, I was about to meet the channeler and teacher who had helped Sam get in touch with the Source and who was helping me to make breakthroughs of my own.

He was met by a kind of reverential silence when he finally entered the room. He was a very large man with gray hair and a gray beard. He welcomed us to the workshop and began by inviting us to take a new look at the Bible. In a neatly diagrammed lecture, Solomon made it clear that the exclusivity of traditional Christianity was inconsistent with the real metaphysical teachings of Christ. The Bible had to be properly understood if it was to have any true spiritual value.

The workshop went well, and as our understandings deepened so did our respect for Solomon. Although he was somewhat aloof and unapproachable, his teachings were remarkable. The days flew by quickly, and we received a broad exposure to Solomon's work. I found the time we spent on spiritual journal writing and dreams to be especially interesting.

During our workshop on dreams, the instructor asked if anyone in the class had an especially unusual dream the previous night. I raised my hand and described my exceptional dream:

> I am walking along a very high trail or path above what looks like the Grand Cannon. The scenery is spectacular, and the colors are brilliant. The trail winds along dangerously close to the edge of the canyon.

*As I wander off the trail toward the edge of the canyon,
the earth suddenly splits off, and I feel myself losing my
footing. I start to fall into the depths of the canyon. I
quickly scramble back to solid ground and eventually get
back on the trail where I join a small group of people
who are listening to a man reading to them from a book
as they walk along together.*

When I finished, the instructor used it as an example in teaching the class. She stated that sometimes in a group one person dreams a dream for the whole group. She said I might have had that kind of dream.

After spending a great deal of time discussing the various images in the dream, we generally agreed that my dream was a warning dream, not only for me but for the whole group—that when we step off the spiritual path there can be great danger. We agreed that the group on the path was our class and that the book being read was the "Good Book" (Bible). The Solomon teachings would help us understand those truths. Looking back on my dream years later, I would see that one element of the dream was never discussed: *why* the dream had me actually stepping off my spiritual path.

In another class, we all sat in the dimly lit room with a partner. Going within and trying to contact the Source through our own higher self, we actually did a reading for the person we were with. When it was my turn to do the reading for my partner, I had no idea what I was saying, but I managed to tell her things that she apparently related to. I wasn't sure if I was channeling or just rambling, but words were definitely streaming out of my mouth. I remember listening to everyone doing readings in the near dark. It reminded me of séances I had seen in the movies.

Near the end of the training, we gave our presentations. I gave an impassioned talk on realizing the ideal of Zorba the Buddha. Drawing on Rajneesh and others, I urged that we all strive for authenticity in our lives, drop our false facades and assumed pretensions, extend love and forgiveness to everyone, celebrate life at all times, and always hang onto the reality of our inner joy.

I had been nervous about the presentation, knowing that it would be videotaped and seriously critiqued, so when I received positive feedback on it I was pleased. Maybe I really could be an effective teacher someday!

Somewhat high from the good reviews, I was surprised to see Sam looking on edge. His talk had not gone well, and he appeared thrown by the attention I was receiving. He seemed to be struggling as his protégé moved out from under his wing. I could sense a new feeling of competition in him, and it made me uncomfortable. In our early morning runs, I had also noted some inconsistencies in his spot readings. I wasn't sure who I was listening to, Sam or the Source. Suddenly Sam was becoming all too human.

At the end of the two weeks, everyone had their personal interview with Paul Solomon. Knowing that people spent huge amounts of money to get readings from Solomon, we considered our time with him to be special—although it was not a reading. We all looked forward to the feedback he would give us on our performance in the last two weeks and in evaluating our abilities as potential teachers.

I was eager as I was ushered in for my interview. However, although Solomon said that he saw me traveling around as a spiritual teacher, he made *no* mention of my doing anything for his organization. Sam and I had talked of trying to start a northern California ILC Center, but Solomon didn't seem to be interested. I was extremely disappointed and knew that Sam would be, too.

Later, Sam and I discussed Solomon's apparent lack of interest in working with us. We tried to be positive, but we both felt bitterly rejected. We tried to rationalize our disappointment, but it didn't work. Somewhat miffed, we jogged around the city doing spot readings, trying to find out from the Source what had gone wrong.

But, all in all, the conference had been worthwhile, and we still maintained high respect for Solomon and his teachings. Maybe in the coming months things would change, and they would decide to start a northern California Center. In the meantime, we would move on with our spiritual lives.

4

Because Sam and his family were driving down to Florida before heading west, I decided to hop a ride with them and visit my brother and his wife. I called my brother before we left and told him we would be there in a week or so.

Traveling through the South in Sam's enormous Southwind motor home, we stopped at Appomattox and Mother Earth Village before heading into the Great Smokey Mountains. The scenery was beautiful, but the sardine-can lifestyle in the motor home proved to be a test for all of us. My presence in the motor home seemed to increase the tension Sam and I had begun to feel in our friendship. The lessons were so hot and heavy at times that we came to describe the motor home as "The Rolling Mystery School."

Wanting to surprise my brother on his birthday, we managed to get there just in time for the "quiet" birthday dinner his wife had planned for the evening. Before she knew it, she had the Rolling Mystery School in her driveway and the California contingent for dinner. With people going this way and that, and the two boys in and out of the bathroom with diarrhea, the idea of a quiet birthday was out the window.

That night at dinner, I watched Sam dominate the conversation with talk about spiritual things. Using metaphysical catchwords and trying to act as a spiritual advisor to another dinner guest, he was embarrassingly insensitive to the needs and interests of the others at the table. I realized that I had never been around Sam in a non-metaphysical setting, and I was surprised by the way he was acting. He *had* to talk about spiritual things. I was sure that my brother, his wife, and my brother's friend were not interested in higher selves or channeled readings. They wanted to eat their turkey dinner and have a few laughs.

As Sam talked on and on, I wished that the Source would tell him to shut up. But it didn't, and there was an unevenness to the meal that made me feel uneasy. I was with my brother and his wife for the first time in a couple of years, and all we were doing was listening to Sam. Then the already stilted evening was completely ruined when the toilet backed up and started overflowing all over the bathroom floor. By that point my brother's wife had had it. She had rolled with the extra company and even Sam's extrasensory insensitivity, but the toilet overflow did it. My brother's birthday celebration was now an official disaster.

We all went out into the front yard hoping we'd be able to find the clogged sewer line. As my brother dug here and there, Sam got his divining rod from the motor home and started pacing around the front yard, trying to zero in on the sewer line.

With his divining rod hovering over a particular part of the lawn, Sam told my brother that he thought he'd found the line and recommended that he dig in that spot. Shaking his head and looking at me in disbelief, my brother's face said it all as he asked me incredulously, "Is this guy for real?"

I told him that I knew it looked weird, but Sam was good at this kind of thing. I suggested digging where Sam was pointing his rod.

My brother did, but it was not the spot. When Sam found a new location, my brother dug again but to no avail. After this happened several times, my brother was understandably upset. Thanks to Sam, his front yard was getting all dug up, and there wasn't even a hint of the elusive sewer line.

Still circling around with his divining rod, Sam stopped for a moment to do a reading on what had gone wrong. But my brother's patience was nearly exhausted, and he suggested that we all go to bed and try again in the morning. The next day my brother found the sewer line, no thanks to Sam.

Later, as my brother and I drove to his softball game I could see that he was really uptight. "Warren, I'm glad you came to visit, but I can't stand your California_____!"

Acknowledging the metaphysical talk and general uproar that had swept into his house since our arrival, I told him that I was really sorry. We certainly fit the stereotype of crazy Californians, and maybe we were. Once he had vented his feelings, though, he quickly forgave me—even inviting me to stay for another week. Sam and I definitely needed a break from each other, and my brother's invitation was the perfect out. I found it impossible to imagine traveling another mile with Sam and the Rolling Mystery School.

Sam wasn't too happy when I told him that I was going to stay another week. When I saw that his feelings were hurt, I felt bad, but I knew it was best for all of us.

As they drove away the next day, I couldn't help but reflect on Jeremy's warning a number of months back and wondered if Sam and I were starting to move in different directions. Certainly on this trip I had begun to see him in a different light. Although I knew I still had more lessons to learn with him, I could tell that things had changed between us significantly. It was time for me to start using my own Source rather than his.

I had a good visit with my brother and his wife. He thought I was pretty extreme, but he had a good sense of humor about everything—once Sam was safely out of town. He was amused that I recorded my dreams, and he thought it was strange that I found synchronistic meanings to things. It was preposterous to him that I actually believed a song on the radio could magically reflect the essence of what we were thinking or what was going on in our lives. He thought my "radio readings" were bizarre, and one day he decided to call my bluff. As we drove down the street, he said, "Okay, let's get our radio reading for the day." He smugly flipped on the radio, and neither of us could believe it when we heard the Hollies singing "He Ain't Heavy, He's My Brother." In the midst of our laughter, my brother learned the meaning of cosmic humor.

At the end of the week when my brother dropped me off at the airport, I promised that the next time I came I would leave my California friends behind. I thanked him for putting up with everything and then ran to catch my plane.

After a short visit to a friend in New Orleans, I finally headed back to California. Flying across the country, I thought about the events of the last month. The Teachers Training. The meeting with Solomon. Traveling with Sam and his Rolling Mystery School. And, of course, the visit with my brother and his wife. As I tried to put things into perspective, I looked forward to getting back home and telling Joy about all of my adventures. And as I thought of her, I realized that I had missed her a great deal.

Ten

More Than Friends

Almost as soon as I got home, I met with Joy. I explained to her that Sam and I had started getting testy with each other and being together day in and day out had worn down both of us. I told her that I could feel myself wanting to back away and be less dependent on him for spiritual support. I was determined to put some space between us, at least for a while, and if our friendship was to survive, it would have to be more of an equal relationship.

Joy understood my feelings about Sam, and she wanted to hear about the Teachers Training and the rest of my trip as well. Because we hadn't seen each other for more than a month, we talked on and on into the evening. The usual flow was still there, as was the ever-present mutual respect for each other's spiritual journey. I knew she had become my closest friend and that no one understood me or cared about me the way she did. She had a soft, peaceful, meditative nature, and I always felt a profound sense of calm when I was with her.

In the coming days and weeks, I saw more and more of Joy as we grew closer on many levels. We met at her house or mine and talked about everything. We also continued to bump into each other everywhere. I would be driving through town and see her on her bike. I would pull over, and we'd stand and talk for a long time, oblivious to the cars and people around us.

As the days rolled by, Joy and I sensed that our relationship was moving to deeper and deeper emotional and spiritual levels. Neither of us talked about it, but sometimes a silence in our conversations would say it all.

2

A friend of Joy's who was a traveling psychic shocked us one night when he suddenly turned to us and said, "Get real. You guys are much more than friends. Start dealing with your feelings. Cut the baloney. You have the potential to have the ultimate relationship, but you both have to get past your resistance and fears. You are both scared stiff, but you can't hide out in your friendship forever. In your day-to-day relationship you are avoiding the intimacy of love that you are already experiencing on soul levels."

Joy and I knew he was right. We *were* scared, and for some time we *had* been hiding in our friendship.

Later when Joy and I were alone, it was strange for us to feel awkward and self-conscious with each other. We were in shock from having our feelings so completely exposed. But with everything out in the open, the question was—what were we going to do about it?

What we did was to start talking about our feelings for each other. It was hard at first because we were so used to relating in a particular way, but we began to acknowledge the depth of emotion we felt. We each needed reassurance that we wouldn't lose our special friendship if we "got involved." But it didn't take long to convince ourselves to give it a try, and soon the feelings we had kept inside began to surface.

As our relationship started to bloom, the love we felt for each other went far beyond anything either of us had ever experienced before. Our friendship had established such a foundation of caring and trust that our new romance was immediately strong and true. Because both of us were so totally committed to a spiritual life, it was also strengthened by our mutual desire for God and truth. But even given all of that, it took me a while to get used to the idea that I was now head over heels in love with my very best friend.

3

I spent Christmas in Yosemite with the friend I had visited in New Orleans after seeing my brother. He had flown in to spend the holidays with his family, who had a home in Yosemite near Chinquapin on the way to Glacier Point. We cross-country skied, hung out in a hot tub that looked out at the snow, and had a great time catching up. When I told him about Joy, I could feel a flush of excitement as I described our relationship. My friend said that he was happy for me and that he looked forward to meeting her someday.

On the last day of the year, I drove down to Yosemite Valley and walked around in the large meadow below Yosemite Falls. As I sat beside the Merced River and looked out toward El Capitan, I reflected on what had been a most unusual and amazing year. Meeting Jeremy in Calistoga. Traveling to the Napa Valley to meet Sam the channeler. Going to the Cayce conference at Asilomar. Getting involved in the Course in Miracles group. Flying to Virginia Beach for the Teachers Training. Traveling with the Rolling Mystery School down to my brother's. And now this relationship with Joy. It had been incredible.

As I sat in the meadow in the midst of the spectacular splendor and majesty of Yosemite Valley, I felt grateful for everything and looked forward to what was yet to come.

On my way home from Yosemite I couldn't wait to see Joy again. When I did, it was clear that our longstanding friendship was now definitely a full-blown romance. We were suddenly—almost magically—a couple. We couldn't see enough of each other. We talked about *everything*. Our usual spiritual dialogues were intensified and heightened by our newly expressed emotions that now set the pace. We knew we were meant to be together and that everything was falling into place. One morning I caught myself whistling a tune I hadn't heard in years. The song was "Everlasting Love."

4

Since getting together with Joy, I was seeing much less of Sam. After establishing some much needed space after Virginia Beach, I had reconnected with him, but our relationship was strained. As it turned out, however, I did still have a few lessons to learn from Sam and his Source. One in particular had to do with trusting my own guidance and not the Source's. It happened in the annual Napa Valley Marathon.

Sam and I had registered for the twenty-six-mile race from Calistoga to Napa, but as the day of the run approached, I seriously questioned my physical stamina for the run. Twenty-six miles was a pretty good haul, and I wasn't sure my body was up to it. My regular running had been much shorter distances. Wanting to get my own guidance on the matter, I wrote down the following question in my dream journal before going to bed one night. "What about my running in the Napa Marathon?"

As I turned off the light, I honestly believed I would have a dream that would help me know what to do. I had my dream journal on the night stand and my mini tape recorder ready to go under my pillow. Sure enough, in the middle of the night when I woke up out of a deep sleep, I remembered that I'd had a dream about a run. I turned the tape recorder on and described the dream in detail. The next morning I transcribed it into my journal:

February 28, 1983—Taking Something I Don't Have
It is the day of the race, and I am running around at the last minute looking for some whole milk. All the runners have whole milk that they are to drink before the race to help them . . . the one that I have is sour. I am looking around in cars to see if anyone has any . . . I am also aware that I shouldn't be taking something from someone else . . . I also remember that I forgot my Guarana [Herbalife fast energy product]. Can't find my way to the start of the

race . . . Wonder if I'll be able to run . . . Upstairs I bump
into Terry Jennings [former fraternity brother, who was
overweight and out of shape] . . . And another guy from
the Delt House . . . I am running around trying to find
the starting line, knowing that I am already expending
energy. Rick [friend who is in really good shape] meanwhile is all squared away with his milk and Guarana and
lined up to start . . . Dream ends as I am still trying to
find the start of the race.

I had asked for guidance on whether to run the Napa Valley
Marathon, and the answer from my dream seemed to be a definite
no. What else could I conclude? The dream was so explicit that I believed I would be a fool to go against it. I told Sam about my dream
and that I had decided not to run. He tried to change my mind,
but I stood firm. When I saw how disappointed he was, I told him
that I would run the first five miles to help him warm up, but then
I would drop out.

The day of the race came, and it was a beautiful day. The morning was crisp and clear as all the runners gathered for the start of the
race. Sam again tried to talk me into running the whole race, but I
told him I was staying with my dream.

The gun sounded, and hundreds of runners shot out into the
Calistoga countryside. As Sam and I ran together, I looked out on
the fresh grassy hills in the distance. The sun was out, the sky was
blue, and it was a truly magnificent day for a marathon run. Sam
must have read my thoughts because he mentioned what a nice day
it was and he wondered if I might change my mind and run the
whole race. I assured him that I trusted my dream and wasn't about
to go against my guidance, and I would appreciate his dropping the
subject. He became very quiet.

After a mile or so, he commented on how strong I looked and
again on what a perfect day it was for running a long- distance race.
I told him that I looked strong because I was in great shape for

short runs. And yes, it was an incredible day, but I wasn't about to let emotional or situational factors get in the way of the guidance I had received. But I was wavering. The fact of the matter was I *did* feel strong. It was a beautiful day. And I had always wanted to run a marathon.

"Maybe we should do a reading," Sam suggested, sensing my weakness.

"No, Sam! I already have my *own* reading, and my lesson is to trust myself!" My words rang with authority, but Sam didn't miss a beat.

"But what if your dream isn't really from your higher self? What if your dream is from your lower self? Maybe the dream is reflecting your fear of failure. You never know. We could check and see!"

And in that telltale moment I flinched and doubted my dream. What if my dream *had* come from subconscious fears and not from my higher self? It was a possibility. Not knowing what else to do, I reluctantly deferred to Sam.

"Okay, Sam. Go ahead and do a quick spot reading. But it had better be the Source and not you."

So as we ran along with hundreds of other runners into the Napa Valley, Sam mentally prepared himself to do a reading on my dream. I had to smile. Edgar Cayce and Paul Solomon had to "go under" to do their channeling, but here was Sam ready to do a reading in the middle of a marathon.

Soon the Source was ready, and as we raced almost exactly in step together the Source answered my question, "What about my running in the Napa Marathon?"

"We would say that you are definitely responding to your subconscious fears and that your dream was not from your higher self. You have the ability to finish the race."

As soon as I heard the reading I wanted to kick myself for letting Sam do it. Now I was confused. Should I go with Sam's reading or my dream?

When I thought about it, I couldn't imagine not finishing the race. Sam's Source was probably right. Maybe my fears had gotten the best of me. So I overruled my dream.

"Okay, Sam. You win. I am going to be positive and know that I'll finish the race." There. I'd made the decision.

Sam tried not to betray his glee, but he was thrilled. With the decision finally out of the way, we picked up our pace and moved out into the heart of the Napa Valley. We had twenty-one miles to go.

I managed to finish the race. I even came in under four hours, which wasn't bad. I wore my purple T-shirt proudly. But what I didn't know as I walked away from the finish line was that I would be severely emotionally and physically drained for almost a month. I ended up paying a heavy price for going against my dream and following the advice of the Source. When I thought back to my dream, I realized that it never said I couldn't finish the race. It said that it would take something I didn't have—energy. My dream's message was that I was not prepared. On the other hand, Sam's Source was correct when it said that I could finish the race, but it gave no hint of the consequences that would follow.

I hoped this would be my last lesson with Sam's Source. Jeremy's warning still rang in my ears as I realized that Sam the Source and Sam the man sometimes became indistinguishable when he had a vested interest. Suddenly, Sam's Source had gone from being my oracle to my Achilles' heel. When would I learn to trust my own higher self?

Within a matter of months, Sam was out of my life. I still cared about him, but, like Rajneesh, he became just another passing teacher on my path.

5

Joy, who had also been studying the course, started attending the Tuesday evening *Course in Miracles* group with me. We both liked Frank and Trudy and after several months came to regard them as our spiritual parents. They had a depth of understanding that came from years of study and spiritual practice. We looked forward to the group each week, and as time went by the group got even larger.

We were all impressed by Frank's teaching. He reminded us that we were perfect, sinless, guiltless Sons of God. He also reminded us that love was *all* that we were and not to allow anyone or anything to tell us it was any other way. He was a master teacher, a great metaphysician, and the ultimate positive thinker. And *A Course in Miracles* was his authority. Expressing love at all times was his spiritual creed. An entry from my journal from that period was typical of what we were learning from the Course and the Course group:

> March 3, 1983—Course in Miracles lesson for the day: Forgiveness is the key to happiness. I will awaken from the dream that I am mortal, fallible and full of sin, and know I am the perfect Son of God.[2]

Thanks to the affirmational lessons of *A Course in Miracles*, we were mentally eliminating illusions of fear or darkness that might interfere with our true perception.

6

Joy and I were very happy in our new ultimate friendship that included all the trappings of a storybook romance. We never tired of each other and rarely argued or had a cross word. In almost every respect, our life seemed right on track and wonderfully fulfilling.

In the spring, Joy enrolled in a local massage certification program and was certified as a practitioner by summer. By that time, I was fully committed to our spiritual pursuits and had resigned my job at the social service agency where I had been working for the last five years.

Both Joy and I were now ready to start working in the holistic health field. We were both certified as massage practitioners, and I hoped to eventually become a spiritual counselor. Joy established her own therapeutic massage practice in what was now our canyon home. As soon as she started advertising in the local paper, people began streaming in. It was exciting to watch her get her practice going, and I was surprised by how confident and self-assured she was with her clients.

While Joy got her business up and running, I began to organize a series of one-day workshops that would be offered to the local community. The workshops were set up for the fall and would be our attempt to bring new spiritual ideas to our area.

It was exciting to have reached the stage where we were finally doing spiritual work. We felt that our lives were now committed to God, and we wanted to create a reality for ourselves that would allow us to continue in the metaphysical field. We wanted to share with others what we had learned already and were continuing to learn. Life seemed especially sweet as we stepped out on our own in faith.

Eleven

The Book in the Bookstore

As summer wound down, Joy's massage business was still growing, and I continued to prepare for the upcoming series of
workshops. I also went into San Francisco to explore the possibility
of updating an inner city resource guide I had written when I was
working for Traveler's Aid. I told Joy to be careful as I said good-bye.

When I returned the next week, Joy greeted me with a startling
account of a strange and frightening incident that had happened on
the very day I had left on my trip. Earlier in the day she had worked
on several new clients, and then in the afternoon, feeling unusually
tired, she lay down in our study at home to rest for a few minutes.
While in a very relaxed state, but not asleep, she said she suddenly
felt her spirit leave her body, and at the same time she could feel an
awful, sinister male presence in the room that seemed to be zeroing
in on her.

Terrified, she summoned all of her strength and willpower as
she tried to fend off the presence, but with no success. She quickly
understood that she was way over her head in some kind of intense
struggle that was spiritual in nature and that the entity had the up-
per hand. She felt that in some insidious way the presence was trying
to "claim" her. She didn't know why she knew that, but she did.

Still lying on the bed and unable to get up or move, she was
amazed at how strong and powerful the entity was. Her spirit and
the entity were in a terrifying confrontation, and her own determination and willpower were no match for this adversary. In a
last-minute, desperate plea she silently called out to God for help,
and slowly, gradually, the entity began to back off and finally went
away.

With her spirit back in her body, she lay exhausted on the bed, bewildered and desperately shaken. A glance at the clock told her she had been out of her body for about two hours. Joy assured me that it was no dream and that she had been wide awake during the entire incident.

I was dumbfounded. The encounter sounded like something out of the Twilight Zone. I didn't pretend to understand it, and neither did she. When I asked her if she had any idea what had happened, she said she didn't have a clue. Although I had no frame of reference for what she told me, I trusted her account. I believed her and felt in my heart that what she had described really happened on some level. When I asked her why she hadn't called me in San Francisco, she said she knew that I would have come home because I'd be so worried. She was right.

The fact that neither of us understood what had happened made it even more frightening. When we tried to fit it into our spiritual belief system, we came up with a number of stock metaphysical explanations. Joy had already wondered if she had actually created the situation herself by projecting some inner fear out into the universe and then experienced it as an entity that seemed to be outside herself. We also wondered if she was trying to teach herself a lesson in affirming and asserting her own personal power and strength. But no matter what we came up with, one thing was certain—the entity had been frighteningly real.

After discussing the incident for several days and trying to figure it out, we finally dismissed it as something we could not understand. Maybe she *had* created or attracted this thing to herself as a lesson in assertiveness. Maybe she was looking into a sort of metaphysical mirror and had freaked herself out as she saw the projected image of her inner fears.

2

A few weeks after the successful completion of our workshops and two months after her out-of-body experience, Joy was giving a scheduled client a massage. He had come once before a couple of months back. The massage seemed to be going well when suddenly she sensed that she was being watched and became uneasy. She looked at the client and was struck with stark terror when she saw a twisted smile on his face and a strange look in his eyes. She shuddered and felt the hair on her arms standing on end. In that moment, she knew he was the one behind her spiritual attack. In horror she recalled having worked on him the day of the encounter. She also remembered that after the attack, when she had asked herself what was going on, an image of his face had flashed through her mind. But it was such a fleeting picture, and it had seemed so improbable that she had immediately let it go. Little did she know that had been her answer.

Trying to be nonchalant, she finished the massage. Only when his car was completely out of sight was she able to let down her guard. But she remembered that the attack had come after his massage. Would he try it again today? She would have to remain on alert, and, no matter what, she would not lie down.

He did try again. Within an hour of the massage she was completely drained of energy. It reminded her exactly how she had felt the first time. And in the wake of the drained feeling came the same spiritual presence with its aura of evil. However, this time, because she was alert, she was not pulled out of her body, and the presence did not remain long.

There was now absolutely no doubt in Joy's mind who the spiritual intruder was. When Joy told me all about the client and that she had been attacked after seeing him, I was in complete agreement with her decision to never give him another massage. But the questions in both of our minds still remained—who was he, and what was he doing in our lives?

3

About a month later, the same man called again for a massage. Joy was feeling particularly strong and somewhat impulsively scheduled him—thinking that the universe was testing her to see if she could stand up to the challenge. She still viewed the situation as an assertiveness test and believed it was important for her to meet the lesson head-on. Joy figured that if she passed the test she wouldn't have to deal with it anymore. Anyway, she reasoned, if she avoided her fears they would probably double back and confront her in some other way.

When she told me she had scheduled a massage for this man, I was understandably upset. But I was reluctantly convinced by her reasoning and the strength of her conviction.

However, on the morning of the scheduled massage she was no longer feeling confident, and we both found ourselves second-guessing her decision. At one point she even considered canceling the appointment, but when it came down to it, she still saw it as a test. Wanting to honor her decision—dangerous as it was—but extremely uncomfortable about it, I insisted that I be in the office next door during the massage. Joy had moved to a new downtown office, and there was a door between hers and the adjoining office. I would come bounding in at the slightest hint of trouble.

By the time we got downtown, she was determined not to let the man intimidate her in any way and to directly confront him about his out-of-body harassment. I assumed my position in the office next door.

Joy told me later that as soon as he came in she asked him to sit down. She wasted no words in telling him straightforwardly, "I know what you are doing, and if you drain me one more time I will never give you another massage!"

Feigning innocence, he pretended that he didn't understand what she was talking about and refused to admit to anything. During the massage, which went well, Joy said she could feel that the man's spirit was out of his body, but it seemed to have no effect on her or what she was doing. After the massage, he confirmed what she had been sensing when he surprisingly volunteered that he had been out of his body during most of the massage. He told her it had been a great massage and that she had given him so much energy he wanted to give some of it back to her. He laid his hands on her shoulders and made an odd squinting gesture with one eye. Joy instinctively pushed him away and authoritatively said, "No!"

Rebuffed, he stormed out of her office. Several minutes later, she saw him coming out of the restroom still looking extremely angry. She sensed that he knew she would never give him another massage.

As she recounted the interaction, I was relieved that she had been able to get out of the situation so smoothly. Joy was not drained that day. Maybe she had finally passed the test and learned her lesson. We were both pleased with the results of her assertiveness. She felt triumphant.

But her victory didn't last long. The next morning, while I was taking a long bicycle ride, the presence returned, and she couldn't do anything to make it leave. Only after a couple of difficult and extremely unpleasant hours did it finally go away. Joy now realized that the man was very proficient in astral projection, and he was continuing to use it in a negative way.

I was agitated when I learned that the presence had returned. I was relieved that Joy was okay, but we were both deeply troubled by what was happening. "Who is this guy, and what is he up to?" we kept asking.

In the succeeding days, Joy was spiritually attacked repeatedly—always feeling the same awful presence. She was convinced that he was unleashing his anger on her for standing up to him. I never

sensed the presence myself, but I learned to discern it by the no-
ticeable oppression that would come over joy. She became dull and
drowsy, and her speech slurred. It was as if her senses were being
jammed, and she was in a strange slow motion. When I asked if she
was feeling the man's spirit around her, she would answer yes.

I would try to talk her through the oppression and do whatever
I could, but nothing seemed to work. We tried every metaphysical and spiritual technique we had ever learned—we repeated our
Course in Miracles lessons, did visualizations, prayed as best we knew
how, sent the spiritual intruder blessings, and kept the whole situation surrounded in white light—but none of it had any effect. We
had to wait it out. The spiritual presence was calling the shots.

4

Within a week of the new attacks, Joy and I called Frank and
Trudy and arranged for a special meeting. We were concerned about the continual spiritual oppression and had exhausted
all of our metaphysical solutions. We were definitely in over our
heads and needed help.

We arrived at their house early in the evening. Joy described
the incident which had taken place when I was in San Francisco and
traced the development of the attacks up to the present moment.
She described the massage client, his usual modus operandi, and the
accelerated attacks since the last massage.

She also explained that we had repeatedly applied our *Course
in Miracles* lessons, such as: "There is nothing to fear," "In my de-
fenselessness my safety lies," and "I could see peace instead of this."[3]
We explained that we had gone through all of our metaphysical
techniques, but nothing had worked. After recapping everything,
we looked at Frank expectantly. We desperately needed his spiritual
expertise.

Frank had listened carefully to what we were saying, but he
made it clear that he agreed with the Course's metaphysical teaching

that evil was only an illusion and that the experience was probably something Joy was working out within herself. As an afterthought, he said he had heard of some unusual cases like ours and that maybe it would be good to do a "treatment."

Frank suggested that the four of us get in a small circle and hold hands. He instructed us to visualize sending light to the man. After "the treatment" we stood silently for several minutes and then dropped our hands. Frank said our visualization should help.

As we got ready to go home, I wondered out loud if there was anything else we could do. In response, Trudy spoke right up and said the strangest thing. "Put on the full armor of God and stand fast against the wiles of the devil!"

We were all caught completely by surprise, and I asked her, "Trudy, what in the world are you talking about?"

"Ephesians 6:10. It's in your Bible. We wrestle not against flesh and blood but against spiritual wickedness in high places." She was now looking at us with wide-eyed conviction.

"Trudy," I said, "*A Course in Miracles* doesn't even believe in darkness or a devil." I still couldn't understand what she was saying.

"I don't care what it says, the devil is real!" she said with absolute determination.

I looked to Frank for clarification. He was our *Course in Miracles* expert, and here was his wife talking about the devil and the powers of darkness. Frank chose not to openly contradict his wife. "Aw, Honey," was all he said. "Come on now."

"I'm sorry, Frank. There is a devil." Looking squarely at Joy and me, she said, "Read Ephesians!"

On the way home, Joy and I agreed that what Trudy had said was pretty wild. But we both respected her, so when we arrived home we got our Bible out and looked up the passage in Ephesians she had mentioned. I read it to Joy.

> Finally, my brethren, be strong in the Lord, and in the
> power of his might. Put on the whole armour of God,

that ye may be able to stand against the wiles of the devil. For we wrestle not against flesh and blood, but against principalities, against powers, against the rulers of the darkness of this world, against spiritual wickedness in high places. (Ephesians 6:10-12)

I rolled my eyes, thinking, *You've got to be kidding.* I looked at Joy for her reaction. She didn't know what to think. We both agreed that it must have had something to do with Trudy's church background. She was probably still hanging on to something from her past. But neither of us doubted that she had our best interests in mind.

However, in spite of Frank's "treatment," the spiritual attacks continued. We were now convinced that they were much more than a manifestation of our own projected fears. There was an external element to the oppression that was not being addressed by our metaphysical belief system. We wished someone could tell us what was happening.

As Christmas neared, we were glad to have an excuse to get out of town for a while. By traveling down to visit Joy's mom in Manhattan Beach for the holidays, we hoped that we would leave the evil presence far behind. But we quickly learned that was not to be the case.

5

Joy's mom had made all sorts of festive holiday preparations for our visit. She had spent hours cooking and baking and even had a Mexican dinner waiting for us after our long drive. It was nice to be on vacation.

However, within a day or so of our arrival in Manhattan Beach, Joy was oppressed again. We could hardly believe it. The distance made no difference. And to make matters even worse, Joy's mom was aware that something was wrong, and she started asking a lot of questions. It was pretty awkward for me because it was the first time I had met her mother, and I wondered if she thought it was my fault. I knew she was concerned about our spiritual interests and reacted strongly against our meditation and "New Age" music. Maybe she thought Joy's problem stemmed from our preoccupation with metaphysical things.

Joy and I tried to explain to her about the massage client and the strange things that had happened, but even we could hear how crazy it must have sounded. She probably thought we were both a bit "out there."

A few days later while Joy was visiting with a friend, I drove down to Hermosa Beach and went to the Either/Or Bookstore to look through their huge metaphysical section. I found myself drawn to a book in the healing section titled *The Beautiful Side of Evil*, by a woman named Johanna Michaelsen.

I had never heard of the book or the author. With all the "evil" we had been dealing with, I wondered if the book had any practical information that could help us. I started to read through it.

I was immediately interested by parallels I saw between the author's life and Joy's. Johanna, like Joy, had been intuitive and supernaturally sensitive to the spirit world from an early age. I found myself caught up in her story and realizing I would be there for a while sat down on the floor and made myself comfortable. I was way back in the corner of the store, well out of anybody's way. I continued reading.

Johanna had been interested in a number of metaphysical areas through the years, including yoga, Silva Mind Control, and spiritual healing. In fact, her progressive involvement in spiritual pursuits eventually resulted in her becoming an apprentice to a psychic healer in Mexico City. She worked with a woman named Pachita, who went into a trance state so that a spirit guide named Hermanito could work through her. He used her body to direct and effect miraculous healings of the many people who came to her for help.

Johanna witnessed miracle after miracle through the psychic healings, and she was happy to dedicate her life to God that way. She believed she was doing God's work and looked forward someday to being a direct channel for Hermanito also.

But some things happened that made her question Hermanito. And as she tried to sort through what was going on with Hermanito and the psychic healings, she began to come under spiritual attack. Her eventual solution for dealing with the spiritual attack was definitely different. Although I had never heard anyone seriously consider what she suggested, I was open to anything that worked. Her story had such a ring of truth that I found myself believing in her words. As I sat on the floor, I started taking notes on everything that seemed to be important.

Engrossed in the book, I was suddenly confronted by a disturbed man whom I had seen on the streets several days earlier. His face was contorted and his voice angry and intimidating. *"Are you going to buy that book?! What are you doing with that book? Are you going to buy it or what?!"* He was furious.

There I was, reading about a woman who had learned to deal with spiritual attack when I suddenly found *myself* under attack. Why was he so upset with me? And why was he so concerned about whether or not I bought the book? It was strange, to say the least.

I could feel my heart pounding. I knew that I was in an extremely vulnerable position on the floor with the angry man towering over me. Choosing not to stand up to avoid provoking him even further, I asked him as calmly as I could if he worked in the store. When he said no, I explained politely that what I did or didn't do was really none of his concern. Realizing that I wasn't going to be intimidated by him and seeing that he was fast becoming the center of attention, he gave me one long icy glare before he turned abruptly and walked out of the store in a huff.

It took me a minute or two to pull myself together. It was as if the evil I had been reading about had suddenly walked into the store. And although it seemed weird, I had to ask myself if it was possible that "evil" was being exposed in the book. And was it possible that "evil" knew I was reading about it? Most frightening of all, was it possible that "evil" could pull a disturbed man off the street and into the bookstore to try to keep me from reading this book?

When I finally finished the book, I put all my notes in my day pack and left the store with new resolve. We now had an entirely new approach to our problem. It was an approach I didn't fully understand, but it had worked for Johanna. And though I didn't know why, I believed her. As wild as her account was, I somehow knew it was true. I was anxious to try her suggestion.

I didn't say anything to Joy about my new findings. But the next morning when she became oppressed, I saw my opportunity to apply what I had learned. I asked Joy if we could go out to her mom's backyard. I told her that I wanted to try dealing with the problem in a different way.

As we sat in the yard, I could see from Joy's face that the presence was particularly strong. I spoke to her as gently and reassuringly as I could and told her not to be afraid. What I was going to try was new, and I thought it would help.

Reading from my notes the exact words that I had taken from Johanna's book, I firmly addressed the presence. "Satan, in the name of Jesus Christ of Nazareth, I command you to be gone! I forbid your presence here. I claim the protection of the blood of Jesus upon us. Go where Jesus sends you!"[4]

Woooosh! Joy's face cleared immediately. The oppression was gone. Joy felt the man's presence leave instantly—as if he had no choice. We were both amazed and deeply impressed.

"What was that?" Joy asked in wonder.

"I'm not sure," was all I could say. "But it has something to do with Jesus and a victory He won over evil on the cross of Calvary. Satan seems to represent the sum of all evil, and that evil was somehow mysteriously defeated when Christ died on the cross. I don't pretend to understand, but it's all written in the Bible, I guess."

Whatever the case, we realized we had just come to a sudden and dramatic understanding that there is something incredibly powerful about calling on the name of Jesus.

As Joy and I walked back into the house, we had no idea that Johanna Michaelsen had just planted a land mine in the middle of our spiritual path.

Twelve

The Mad Magician

During our remaining days in Manhattan Beach, whenever the spiritual presence reasserted itself, Joy and I simply called on the name of Jesus and the presence left immediately. We didn't pretend to understand what we were doing, but we knew it worked. Commanding in the name of Jesus apparently carried great power in the spirit world. We were amazed that the presence left every time we called on His name. Nothing in *A Course in Miracles* or any of our other metaphysical teachings had ever talked about this aspect of Jesus.

Although much of what Johanna Michaelsen said in *The Beautiful Side of Evil* was contrary to our beliefs, we were grateful for her help in dealing with the spiritual presence. Too embarrassed at first to buy her book that day at the Either/Or, I had gone back to get it the next day after our positive results. We were surprised that an obviously Christian book with a literal approach to the Bible had made its way into the metaphysical section of the bookstore. We also found it interesting that Johanna's book confirmed what we had recently come to believe ourselves—that there is an unseen, external element of evil that can affect everyday life.

She talked openly about a deceptive spirit world and about how she had been cleverly deceived into accepting evil spirits as her spirit guides. The seemingly radiant and benevolent guides were not at all the loving beings they pretended to be. She even described one evil spirit that said he was "Jesus." It was only when she learned about the real Jesus of the Bible that she was able to see she had been deceived by the false "Jesus." When she had confronted the false "Jesus" spirit guide, he was forced to leave.

I had trouble putting Johanna into my usual Christian box. I certainly didn't accept everything she said, but I couldn't categorically dismiss her either. Her experiences had closely paralleled Joy's, and she was the only one who had been able to help us deal with the evil presence. Though we were thankful for her help, we weren't about to drop down on our knees, confess our sins, and ask Jesus to be our Lord and Saviour.

Johanna did, however, spark something that made us want to start reading the Bible for ourselves. We found it interesting that she had made none of the usual excuses and apologies for the Bible. She believed it was literally God's Word, and, as such, it should have the final say in all spiritual matters.

Joy and I were somewhat embarrassed to realize that in all of our years of spiritual seeking and journeying, neither of us had ever thoroughly read the Bible. In our minds, the literal Bible had been put out to spiritual pasture. Now Johanna was convincing us to check it out more carefully.

So we agreed to read the Bible in addition to *A Course in Miracles*. Maybe each would help to bring out things in the other that we hadn't understood. By reading the Bible, perhaps we would get an even bigger picture of what A Course in Miracles was trying to teach us. In the past we had regarded the Course as the final word. But now we were being persuaded that there was value in reading God's Word, too.

2

Within several weeks of our return home after the holidays, the spiritual presence of the massage client, which had been in and out of our lives for more than three months, was completely gone. It seemed that in the face of our newly learned prayers and commands he had finally given up.

As the new year unfolded, we returned with renewed vigor to our day-to-day lives. Joy returned to her holistic massage practice.

While she was busy at work, I started to fix up the office next to hers so that I could do spiritual counseling and have a place for any workshops we might do in the future. We were both excited—the office building on Main Street was starting to shape up as a potential alternative holistic health center.

As the days rolled by, my energy was largely spent in removing years of paint from the windows and doors and in doing everything I could to get the office back to its original charm. I spent many peaceful hours fixing it up. Lost in thought above the hustle and bustle of Main Street below, I would only occasionally be jolted back to reality by the blast of a car horn, the over-amplified sermons of our local town evangelist across the way, or Joy popping her head in the door to see how I was doing.

It was also about that time that a friend and I put the finishing touches on a portable puppet playhouse I hoped to use in the community. It was an elaborately reconverted refrigerator carton with inner shoulder straps, a window area complete with stage and curtains, a built-in sound system, and a beautiful red calico cover. It was specifically designed so that I could be mobile as I wandered around hospitals, care homes, and birthday parties giving puppet shows. In the back of my mind I was already writing scripts that would teach children basic metaphysical principles.

In the mornings before heading off to town, Joy and I would read from *A Course in Miracles* and then from the Bible. We were enjoying the combination and found the Bible to be much more readable than we'd ever imagined. We respected this Jesus of the Bible, who traveled around the countryside healing people of their sicknesses and diseases and even casting out evil spirits. Joy and I were both surprised by how much evil Jesus came up against in His ministry and that He took it seriously and dealt with it straight on. That the Bible and *A Course in Miracles* differed so much on the matter of evil continued to trouble us. Why the discrepancy? It was an issue I was always bringing up in the Course group. And it was usually dismissed quickly.

Joy and I had revealed some of our recent experiences, but we could tell that people were growing weary of our talk. They seemed to have no interest in our learning to call on the name of Jesus.

All in all, though, our life was pretty much back to "normal." And Joy and I were thankful for the day-to-day peace we were feeling, now that the presence was finally gone. We stayed busy at work, took long walks in the canyon, and enjoyed being back on an even keel. Although we hadn't forgotten Johanna's book, it was becoming more of a distant memory as we focused our energies on our everyday lives. As far as we were concerned, our "evil" days were behind us.

3

Beginning in February, we came into almost daily contact with a man we had known from our mutual involvement in the local metaphysical community. He was a familiar presence around town, and we began to see him almost everywhere.

Joy began noticing that whenever she was around him she felt a tremendous uneasiness and discomfort. She found herself watching him closely, not trusting his intentions. She kept thinking, *That peaceful, loving man, who seems to be concerned with personal and spiritual growth is putting on a big front for everyone.*

As intuitive as she was, and as many times as her intuition had proven true in the past, she still second-guessed herself for feeling wary when she was around him. She wondered if something was wrong with her. She tried to let go of her feelings about the man, but each time she saw him her uneasiness seemed to increase.

One morning after we had seen him, Joy told me that in the middle of our conversation with him she had experienced what seemed to be an incredibly strong and powerful alarm going off inside. It seemed to be saying, "Be careful! This man is not who he says he is! Stay away from him!"

From then on, the alarms went off whenever she saw him. She had no idea why she was on such alert. But whenever she tried to push her internal warnings aside, they seemed to get louder.

Joy found the situation especially bewildering because she had known the man for several years and had gotten along well with him. He had always been likeable and friendly, and she had only had a few uneasy moments with him—moments that paled in significance when compared to their positive interactions. But she realized that those flickering tensions in the past were probably early intimations of what she was feeling intensely now.

Soon the alarms moved into Joy's dreams. Some vivid, straightforward dreams issued warnings to watch out for the man and what he was doing. She wrote the dreams in her journal, and as she studied them she could see that some part of herself was clearly telling her that the man was into "the dark side." Her dreams confirmed what she had already been feeling. So we started taking the situation more seriously. But why was Joy picking up on all of this? And what, if anything, did it have to do with her or us?

My feelings on the subject fluctuated. I knew that Joy was extremely intuitive. She had a way of "knowing" and "seeing" things. She was so perceptive and so accurate with her "sixth sense" that I had hidden her last birthday present at a neighbor's house. The night before her birthday, I was awakened by Joy's exclamation, "Oh, it's so beautiful!" When I asked her what was so beautiful, she described the stained glass that I had hidden at the neighbor's, detailing it down to the purple iris framed in the middle.

She had been doing things like that ever since I'd met her. She often knew what I was thinking, when her mother was going to call, if a friend was in trouble, or if someone was coming over. When we were first dating, I told her she could have all the change in my Indian pot if she could guess the correct amount within twenty-five cents. And she had done it. She said the exact figure of $52.50 was the first one that had come to her mind, but she had doubted it and guessed $52.25 instead. She had also "seen" the image of the massage client's face that flashed before her when she had wondered who her spiritual assailant had been last fall but had quickly dismissed it. Her initial intuition about the $52.50 and the massage client's face were two instances when she'd had immediate correct intuitive impressions but doubted herself.

In light of her intuitiveness, I could not discount her feelings about our "friend" downtown. Yet I had crossed paths many times with this man in the last several years, and he hardly seemed the type to be into darkness of any kind. On the contrary, he was generally regarded as spiritual and was even bringing a lot of light to our community.

One day, after another one of Joy's warning dreams, I saw him downtown, and we talked for a while. He was as positive and upbeat as ever. As I walked away, I had to shake my head about Joy's concerns and the so-called warnings. There had to be some other explanation. He was too nice a guy.

But then, almost immediately, I started having dreams about him, too. They had the same general theme about the underlying presence of evil around the man and that he was not who he seemed to be. In one of my dreams he was even referred to as "the mad magician." Was I subconsciously spinning off Joy's unfounded fears with my own piggyback paranoia, or was there truth to all the warnings?

Once I started having my dreams, I also started feeling uncomfortable around him. Joy and I continued to relate to him in our usual manner, but we were starting to exercise an inner watchfulness as we questioned the motives and intentions of this seemingly spiritual man. Was he hiding something? Was Joy's intuition blowing his spiritual cover? Was he threatened by what was happening? The answer seemed to be yes.

As the days went by, each time we saw him the vibes seemed to get more strange. Our encounters were so intense that you could almost feel them crackling in the spiritual airwaves. We were all watching each other, and we all knew that we all knew, but nothing was being said. It was like a game of cat and mouse, and it became more and more certain that something would have to give.

4

On the night of March 4, 1984, I had what I believed to be an extremely significant dream. In the dream, several people who seemed to be spiritually advanced told me that everything I had learned up to that point had been "absolutely elementary." They told me that I had many spiritual openings and I needed to watch out for evil spirits attacking me. One person placed a crucifix in my hand and in so doing seemed to say, "You'd better watch out" and "You'd better hang on to the cross." When I woke up, I was sober. I told Joy about it, and we both agreed it was a grave warning.

A little more than a week later I had another dream, which I recorded in my journal:

> **March 13, 1984—Digging Into the Light**
> I am in a canyon. There are cliffs and walls surrounding me. I am with someone else, and we are furiously digging into the earth to uncover light. The enemy has surrounded us and I feel a slight sense of panic, even fear—but somehow I know that digging into the light is the answer. Running away wouldn't work.

After the dream, I had an even more heightened sense of impending danger. It seemed to connect with our dealings with "the mad magician." What was all this—being surrounded by enemies and a search for light? Why was the mad magician our enemy? And what was this darkness he was into? We didn't have to wait long to get our answers.

Four nights later on March 17, after weeks of dreams and intuitive warnings about the mad magician, it all came crashing down. In the late evening hours, I was startled out of my sleep by an awful evil presence pressing in upon me. I bolted upright and in a horrified, broken voice called out, "Help me, God!"

Joy sprang out of bed in a flash and was immediately by my side. She knew exactly what was going on. Looking directly at me, she addressed the unseen presence, "In the name of Jesus Christ, leave Warren alone!"

And woosh! It was as if a huge weight had been removed from my throat. Whatever the presence was, it left as soon as Joy called on the name of Jesus.

I sat on the edge of the bed still stunned by the suddenness and severity of the spiritual attack and by the fact that the presence had been forced to leave so quickly. "That's amazing," I said. "Something was literally going down my throat, but it left as soon as you addressed it in the name of Jesus!" Now I knew what it had been like for Joy in her mother's backyard.

Joy and I were both unnerved. We stayed up and talked and agreed that, thanks to all our warnings, we hadn't been caught totally by surprise. But it's hard to be fully prepared when everything still seems unreal in the back of your mind. After about a half an hour, we finally went back to sleep.

Almost immediately, Joy was awakened by a spiritual presence. She could hardly speak as it now attacked her throat area. This time I commanded, "In the name of Jesus Christ, I command you to leave!"

When Joy told me the presence had left, we looked at each other in bewilderment. What in the world was going on?

Throughout the night, we were repeatedly harassed by something as it tried to move in on us while we slept. As soon as we became aware of it, we commanded the presence to leave. Although it always left, it seemed to have no hesitation about returning, but only after we had gone back to sleep again. This continued almost all night long.

In the morning we were physically, emotionally, and mentally exhausted. But we made it to work. And we were still on our feet. Barely.

5

We continued to encounter wave after wave of spiritual attack as the mad magician's fury beat upon us relentlessly and mercilessly almost every night. We were convinced that our "friend" was upset because we had seen through his cover and that the spiritual attack was his way of trying to intimidate us. What he hadn't bargained on was our surprisingly solid spiritual defense.

Even though Joy and I knew we were being protected by Jesus, in our spiritual naivete we decided to take additional measures. We put a picture of Jesus by our bed and surrounded it with burning candles. And we started having our dog and cat sleep with us. Sometimes the dog would recoil in fear or growl, tipping us off when something had come. We also slept clutching crosses that Trudy Phillips had loaned us, and the Bible was always by our side or on the bed. We even bought a tape of Christian hymns that we played on our stereo all through the night. We quickly found that we had no trouble relating to, even acquiring a fondness for, "A Mighty Fortress Is Our God," "Onward Christian Soldiers," and "The Battle Hymn of the Republic." To top it off, I bought five new lamps, put the highest watt bulbs I could find in each one, and left them on all night long.

One evening in the midst of the harassment and chaos, I realized that our life was so out of control it was almost slapstick. We had become like the people you see on the late-night movie, raising their crosses against approaching vampires and other evil forces. We were caught in the middle of our own late-night drama. I had to laugh as I listened to the hymns playing on the stereo and watched the candles flicker by the picture of Jesus as we lay there in bed with our cat, our dog, our crosses, and our Bible. For two people who thought we were creating our own reality, we were quite a sight.

Although our props provided some psychological comfort, we knew our protection was not coming from them. It was coming from Jesus. The picture, the crosses, and the Bible reminded us who was helping us, but we recognized that they had no real power of their own. Soon the crosses went back to Trudy, the Bible went back on the shelf, and the picture of Jesus was given to the Salvation Army.

6

One evening as we drove home from the office, Joy told me that she felt led to look up a dream in her journal she'd had more than a year ago. She could not remember who was in the dream or what it was about, but she knew it was important and that it would help us understand what was happening.

When Joy showed me the dream, she told me that because it was in two parts, with one scene shifting to another, she had missed the connection between the man in the first part of the dream and the image of the black magician in the second. I was astounded when I saw that the man in the first part of the dream was none other than the mad magician. It was another compelling warning about our "friend" downtown.

7

Black magician, mad magician, sorcerer, wizard, or metaphysician—it didn't matter what he was called. Everything we were experiencing spelled out the fact that our seemingly nice "friend" was into some not-so-nice things. Joy and I decided that it was time to address the subject directly. We had talked around it for too long. It was time to get everything out in the open. If we addressed him specifically, maybe something would change. At any rate, we wanted to tell him in person that we were aware of what he was doing.

The next time I saw him, I told him we wanted to talk to him about some "serious concerns." He agreed to meet us that day in the downtown park. Later, as we were all about to sit down in a grassy area to talk, a man on the other side of the park screamed an obscenity I had never heard before, using the name of Jesus. With that bitter, ugly denunciation of Jesus ringing in the air, I looked over at the mad magician and watched un believingly as a small spider scampered across the front of his shirt. I thought, *This can't be happening. I must be in the middle of a Stephen King movie.*

Addressing our "friend," I told him that some strange things had been happening in our lives. I held nothing back as I detailed the events of recent weeks, including the spiritual attacks and our mutual conclusion that our trouble was coming from him. I talked about Johanna Michaelsen's book and her discovery that her spirit guides were actually evil spirits. And I told him that we had learned to call on the real Jesus. I was respectful and straightforward. I minced no words and wasted no time.

When I finished, he paused a moment and then thanked me for "sharing." He politely told us that he thought we were projecting our "inner darkness" onto him and that he had nothing to do with our "spiritual problems." Defending his own spirit guides, he told us they were *not* evil spirits. And making a stab at an explanation, he wondered if we were experiencing other people's thought forms, or "elementals" as he called them. It was clear that he was not about to take responsibility for what he was doing.

Joy had been quiet up to that point, but now she had something to say. She looked him squarely in the eye and said matter-of-factly, "I'm not threatened by you or anything that you are doing, and I *know* your spirit guides are not from God. I don't trust what you are saying, and I don't trust your intentions at all."

He quickly made some throwaway remark about our misunderstanding everything and tried to end the meeting on an innocent note. Joy and I might second-guess ourselves later for revealing so much to him, but it seemed the spiritually decent thing to do. At least now everything was out in the open. But there was no doubt about it, his denials had been unquestionably smooth. We wondered what would happen next.

8

When we saw him early the next week, he was anything but cool. He looked pale and haggard and was not his usual social self. We saw an element of desperation in his face, and he appeared somber and uncharacteristically withdrawn—not just around us but with others, too.

Joy and I wondered if our meeting in the park had unnerved him. We knew that our spiritual defenses were throwing a monkey wrench into his modus operandi.

Whatever the case, it seemed clear that a great deal was going on in the spirit world and we would need to stay on our toes. There was so much that we didn't know. But just as we were learning about the reality of black magic and evil spirits, we suspected that our "friend" was also learning some valuable lessons. And one of them was that there is a lot more to Jesus than what you see on TV.

Thirteen

The Ultimate Puppet Show

During our latest wave of spiritual oppression, it had been difficult to listen to our *Course in Miracles* group affirm how perfect everything was in the spiritual realm. We had done our best to explain our recent experiences to them, but, other than Trudy at times, no one believed us. And although nobody came right out and said it, we knew they viewed us as a couple of alarmists.

From the group's perspective, evil was still an illusion, and it was our own fearful, misguided thoughts that were coming back to haunt us. Once we finally learned that there is only love, our problems would disappear—but, of course, that had been our thinking, too, until we found that evil is *not* an illusion. And evil spirits don't respond to affirmations based on the assumption they don't exist.

Joy and I were becoming more and more frustrated with the group—but we kept thinking that sooner or later they would get it and would realize that something had really happened to us, and we weren't just freaking out over nothing. But it didn't happen. Joy and I were aghast that what we were describing was regarded so casually and indifferently by the Course and the group.

But thanks to Johanna Michaelsen and the Bible, many of the puzzle pieces were coming together. Evil *was* real. And our means to combat it came not from ourselves but from calling on Jesus.

Although we still resisted the classical idea of Jesus as our "personal Saviour," we had to admit that in every sense of the term He had been just that. He had saved us from the wiles of the mad magician night after night and had kept us from harm. Never once had He let us down. He was definitely real. And His victory on the cross was real. In no time flat, He had become our best friend.

While we struggled through our trouble and trauma and triumph, it was still business as usual at the Tuesday night Course group. Everyone else charged ahead, talking of love and light and inner peace. In the group's indifference to our plight, Joy and I saw the Course group as the metaphysical equivalent of the complacent church. Their comfort level took priority over their search for truth. And our foxhole reports about the reality of evil were starting to ruin their spiritual good time.

All we wanted was honest, meaningful discussion—not an affirmational deaf ear. We were tired of the Course's "see no evil, speak no evil" attitude, which effectively kept us on a spiritual leash. We couldn't say or do anything in regard to evil that didn't make us look ridiculous to the rest of the group.

It was no use. As far as the group was concerned, Joy and I were way off base. We finally realized that *A Course in Miracles* was not about to be measured by our experiences. Rather, our experiences would always be measured by *A Course in Miracles*. Though I still cared about the Course, I no longer believed it was as perfect as I once thought. When it came to evil, it clearly missed the mark.

Joy and I realized that we were all spinning our wheels. We could have handled the unspoken judgment if we were actually moving forward. But we had become a thorn in the side of the group, and they were becoming a bit of a drag for us, too. We could all forgive each other as much as we wanted, but we were still miles apart on the issues of evil and the authority and power of Jesus. As loving and accepting as we all tried to be with one another, everyone's patience was wearing thin. Sooner or later, something had to give.

At a Course group potluck at the Phillips' house, some of my frustrations came to the surface, and I got into an unexpectedly heated discussion with a woman. She told me I was taking everything too seriously, and I said I didn't think she was taking things seriously enough. As our conversation increased in volume, it became clear that neither of us were experiencing anything remotely resembling the Course's stated objective of inner peace. In effect, each of us was saying to the other, "Get real," but we no longer had an agreed-upon definition of what "real" was. It was a spiritual Catch-22. The woman and I never did resolve our differences, and the potluck ended with frayed nerves and hurt feelings.

Joy and I agreed there was an unresolvable breach within the group and that it was time for us to say good-bye. At the next meeting we told everyone that we were leaving the group. They certainly had a right to study *A Course in Miracles* without all of our persistent questions. We told them that we wanted to get out now while we were all still friends.

There was an awkward silence as we all realized the finality of our decision. Joy and I had been an integral part of the group for a long time. We had seen lots of people come and go. We had been among the most enthusiastic proponents of the Course and its metaphysical—and what was now being called "New Age"—spirituality. So our leaving was a shock. But I knew that if the group was honest, they would admit that although they were sorry we were leaving, it wasn't a moment too soon.

As we hugged everyone good-bye, we felt a sense of frustration that it had to end this way. It was confusing for all of us, but it was probably most bewildering for our friend Taylor. For more than a year, I had been telling her about the Course group and how great it was and that she ought to come and join us. On that night of all nights she had finally come. A look of utter disbelief covered her face as Joy and I said good-bye and walked out the door.

2

It was strange to leave the Course group, but we never looked back. Because of the mad magician, our eyes had been opened to the fact that there was a dark side to life we had never imagined. The issues that had been raised by the massage client had now been compounded by the mad magician. Although we didn't welcome the lessons into our life, we were grateful to be aware of what was going on. Knowing that such things were real and not an illusion had enabled us to effectively confront the evil that was coming at us.

Ironically, the mad magician, rather than blowing our lives apart as he had intended, actually helped to bring Joy and me closer together. Having learned under fire how to call out and pray in Jesus' name, we were surviving the spiritual oppression amazingly well. And like a silver lining in a dark cloud, it was in the midst of the spiritual madness that I finally proposed to Joy. In spite of everything, or maybe because of everything, we were more in love than ever.

I woke up one morning knowing that I wanted Joy to be my wife, and I would propose to her that evening. On my way to work I prayed, "Dear God, You know my heart and You know I want to marry Joy. Please help me to know if it is Your will, too. In Jesus' name, Amen."

I flipped on the radio and could hardly believe my ears. It was Van Halen singing "Jump." When I turned to another station, someone was singing, "You'll be so happy together." And as I switched from station to station, every song on the radio seemed to be about Joy and me. Call it a radio reading, synchronicity, God's will, or my own foolish heart—whatever it was, it was fun. And so it went throughout the day. I was soaring with an ever-present, wonderfully peaceful understanding that proposing to Joy was absolutely and unmistakably the right thing to do.

That night when we got home, I told Joy I wanted to do a special puppet show for her. After setting up my brightly colored portable puppet playhouse in the living room, I climbed inside and got everything together. The stage was set, and my heart was ready. I then performed an impromptu puppet show that culminated in the playing of the wedding march and in one of the puppets handing Joy a dozen red roses, as I stuck my head through the curtains and asked her to marry me. The show was a success, and she gave me a big kiss and agreed to be my wife. It was a special moment. For us to be able to laugh and love and make a lifetime commitment in the midst of all of our trials was a most remarkable and wonderful thing.

3

What a month it had been! The spiritual tornado that hit us on the night of March 17 had set up a rapid progression of events which included near sleepless nights, a confrontation with the mad magician in the park, the end of our participation in the Course group, and our decision to marry. It had been a wild roller coaster as a lifetime of events were compressed into a frighteningly real, incredibly powerful thirty days.

But the ride wasn't over. Far from it. Joy and I still woke up some nights knowing that a spiritual presence was in the room. But when we called upon Jesus and prayed, it always left.

We still saw the mad magician, but our conversation was usually minimal. And Joy and I always prayed carefully after seeing him. We wondered how many other black magicians were walking around, pretending to be nice guys but secretly doing their evil thing.

We continued reading from *A Course in Miracles*, but we were much more enthusiastic about the teachings of the Bible. No longer believing that the Scriptures were outdated and impractical, we had learned from the recent events in our lives that they were quite the opposite. The Bible had helped us meet the challenges of the massage client and the mad magician when nothing else could.

But as much as we were reading the Bible, we didn't pretend to understand everything it said. Sometimes we came upon Scriptures that we just didn't know what to do with. However, we were now praying about the things we didn't understand, rather than pushing them aside or discounting them altogether. Whenever we had trouble with a particular verse or teaching in the Bible, we would ask God to open our eyes and help us see what we were confused about.

And one issue that was hanging us up was the description of a real spirit being named Satan. He was described in the Scriptures as the enemy of God, the one who worked evil in the world and in people's lives.

Since first addressing the evil presence in Joy's mom's backyard that day, Joy and I had regarded Satan as a generic, all-inclusive term for evil, rather than a specific spirit being. Now we weren't so sure. Although we had never given the possibility of his existence a second thought, we had learned enough about evil spirits of late that the idea of their reporting to a spirit leader no longer seemed so out of the question.

As we studied and prayed about the subject, I couldn't help but remember the old "Flip Wilson Comedy Hour" when he played a character named Geraldine who was always blaming everything on the devil. She would say, "The devil made me do it!" and the audience would roar with laughter.

Clearly, the devil has been used as a convenient scapegoat by many, many people through the years. Like Flip Wilson's Geraldine, people have tended to avoid personal responsibility for their own mistakes by projecting them onto the figure of Satan. And untold wars, witch-hunts and other horrors were committed by people who said they were on the side of good, fighting "the devil." Yet even as we understood the projection and displacement which had gone on in Satan's name, we strongly believed that the scapegoating in and of itself didn't mean that Satan couldn't be real.

In the Scriptures, Jesus was constantly dealing with the devil. He was tempted by him, talked to him, taught about him, confronted him, and ultimately defeated him on the cross of Calvary. We asked ourselves, "Was that all symbolic?" The world said yes. The Scriptures said no. The Scriptures warned everyone not to be taken in by the lies of the world. The world warned everyone not to be taken in by the myths of the Scriptures. Round and round it went.

One thing we had to consider at this point was that it was the Scriptures, not the world or our metaphysical/New Age teachings, that had been accurate in describing the reality of evil and evil spirits. Could they now be wrong about Satan? The question was crucial for a number of reasons, not the least of which was the issue of the overall reliability of the Scriptures. If they were wrong on the subject of Satan, then everything else they said was suspect, too. Could we trust the Bible as God's truth if some things in it were untrue? Joy and I had come to believe that the Bible was the first spiritual teaching we could rely on. So far, it hadn't let us down.

Knowing we could no longer depend exclusively on our logical human minds or on our metaphysical understandings, but not completely sure of the Bible, we knew we could depend on God Himself to help us. So we prayed and asked Him to show us the truth about Satan.

In the coming days, God answered our prayer in many different ways. Perhaps the most significant and straightforward was a dream that Joy recorded in her journal.

April 30, 1984—Dream: The Tester

Warren and I are at Mom's house. A man picks us up in his car. He takes us to see many things. This man encompasses the whole planet and knows about all people. He's manifesting to us as a physical person, yet he really isn't one per se. He shows us all destruction, disease, crime, unhappiness, etc.—he's in charge of all the bad in life, yet we're also made aware that there is a positive thing to all of this: It often brings people to seek the almighty God. This man, however, tries to divert people's attention and tests people. He's a powerful guy. He takes us back to my folks' house and leaves us. He has quite a sobering and chilling presence. We are shaking all over—we've been shaken to our senses. That was Satan! We now see life quite differently. Our lives will never be the same.

Especially in that dream, but in other ways, too, we strongly believed God was telling us that the Scriptures stood as truth. Satan was real.

When Joy and I had time to reflect, we realized that we had both spent much more time, thought, and prayer in coming to believe in the reality of Satan's presence than we ever had in believing that he did not exist. We wondered how many people ever stopped to question their assurance that Satan was only a myth. How many people had ever really searched their hearts and prayed about it? We certainly hadn't. But when we did, the answer was clear. We were starting to understand that Satan's ultimate deception had been to convince us that he was not even real. As I thought about it, *A Course in Miracles* with its metaphysical/New Age philosophy was playing right into his hands by claiming that evil was only an illusion.

But Joy was about to take it a step further. Even though I had read Johanna's book and the entire New Testament, I was still so identified with my metaphysical background that I had completely missed the forest for the trees. I had come to understand the reality of evil and spiritual deception, but I had missed the most obvious thing of all. Joy was about to point it out and hand me my biggest shock yet. And when she did, it turned what was left of my metaphysical world inside out and upside down.

Fourteen

The Aquarian Conspiracy

Several days later, Joy finally put into words what she had been feeling for weeks. Gently, but in no uncertain terms, she told me that she didn't think *A Course in Miracles* was from God or that the Jesus of the Course was the real Jesus. As far as she was concerned, all of our metaphysical spirituality was straight out of Johanna Michaelsen's *The Beautiful Side of Evil*. Her words rang with conviction. Although I wanted to protest and say, "No way!" another part of me wondered, *Could it be true?*

I was at a loss for words as I considered the staggering implications of what she was suggesting. Was the same thing happening to us that had happened to Johanna? Was the Jesus of *A Course in Miracles* like her spirit guide—a false Jesus? Was the Jesus who delivered the Course a deceptive spirit that was only pretending to be Jesus? Was it all a part of some elaborate spiritual trap? Was what I had always thought to be a benign and divine supernatural set-up not so benign or divine after all? Was the seemingly outfront "Aquarian conspiracy" a real conspiracy? Had what Bonnie described as "the other side" been just that—the other side? Had we been led away from God in the name of God? Was the deception deeper and darker than we had ever imagined?

It was almost too much to even begin to comprehend. Everything within me fought against the idea. Yet I had read enough of the Bible in the last five months to know that the scenario Joy was suggesting was a real possibility. Had we been able to see the deception in Johanna's life but not in our own? There had been so much coming at us in the last few months—had we failed to put two and two together?

I told Joy that as much as I wanted to tell her she was way off base, I couldn't. Maybe the Course and the Jesus of the Course *were* part of the deception that Johanna and the Bible talked about. But I told her that no matter what she thought might be going on, I wasn't going to be convinced of anything until I could see it all laid out in front of me in black and white, and the only way for me to resolve the question was to sit down with the Course and the Bible and to study it out.

2

For the better part of a week, I holed up in my study with the Course and the Bible. I studied *A Course in Miracles* carefully and spent hours poring over the Scriptures. By the end of the week, my old roll-top desk was covered with notes, file cards, charts, and diagrams. I had dissected the Course and the Bible with a fine tooth comb. And I had found my answers.

My conclusions were inescapable and shocking. *A Course in Miracles* and the Bible were two completely different thought systems that were mutually exclusive and diametrically opposed in every degree! To my utter amazement, *A Course in Miracles* was the Holy Bible turned upside down. The Course had not updated or reinterpreted the Bible—it had completely rewritten it.

I could see that the Course and the Bible were not even remotely related. They were two different gospels. To believe in one was necessarily to disbelieve the other. It was a case of either/or but not both/and. Because the Course and the New Testament were *opposite* teachings, they were by definition *opposed* to each other. Although the Course and our other metaphysical teachings had gone to great lengths to make it look as if they were compatible with the Christ of the Bible, they were not. To be opposite and contrary is to be against. Jesus had made it clear:

He that is not with me is against me. (Matthew 12:30)

I no longer had any doubt that the Course and our other meta-physical teachings were not *with* the Bible's Jesus or the Bible's gospel at all. Their oppositional teachings actually went against everything the Bible's Jesus taught.

If the gospel of the Bible was the real gospel—and I believed it was—then the metaphysical gospel of the Course and the New Age was anti-gospel. If the Christ of the Bible was the real Christ—and I believed He was—then the metaphysical Christ of the Course and the New Age was anti-Christ.

Joy was right. *A Course in Miracles* was not from God. And the Jesus of the Course was not the real Jesus. Who would have ever guessed that the metaphysical/New Age gospel that came in the name of Christ would actually end up denying Christ? As I sat there thinking about how much I had trusted the Course, I felt as if I had just been stabbed in the back by one of my closest friends.

3

During my week of study, the more I compared the differences between the two gospels, the more concerned I became. I could now see that things I had once thought to be minor differences between the Course and the Bible were actually huge differences. And other things that I had accepted as truth in the Course, even six months ago, I now passionately disbelieved. It was during my study that I came to understand just how much the events of recent months had changed my perspective. As I studied the Course, I realized that I no longer believed it at all. Its teachings suddenly seemed hollow, empty, and false.

For some time now, my spiritual teachings had convinced me that I was a sinless, guiltless, perfect Son of God and that I was every bit as much a part of the universal Christ as Jesus or Buddha or anyone else. I had been taught that I was a holy part of God, inherently equal to Christ and that I didn't need to be saved, redeemed, or born again. Because evil was only an illusion, there was no evil to be saved from. I had believed that I was responsible for myself and my world and I was the creator of my own reality.

But as I looked at those "truths" now, I could see that they were not truths at all. What was being taught—no matter how cleverly expressed—stood in stark opposition to the actual teachings of the Bible. Couched in spiritual platitudes, the Course and the New Age, although pretending to be friends of Jesus and the Bible, were really no friends at all. Like Judas, they betrayed Christ in the name of love and with a deceptive kiss.

Jesus warned about false prophets who would come in sheep's clothing—even in His name. His words were concise and clear:

> Beware of false prophets, which come to you in sheep's clothing, but inwardly they are ravening wolves. (Matthew 7:15)

They would look not like an enemy but like someone you could trust, and I was now thoroughly convinced that the Course was a channeled wolf in sheep's clothing that came not to praise the Bible's Jesus but to bury His teachings forever, if that were possible.

In the midst of my study, I started to understand that for a number of years I had been letting my spiritual teachers—most especially the Course—tell me who Jesus "really" was and what His teachings "really" meant. I could see that through my own laziness in never reading or studying the Bible for myself, I had swallowed a false gospel—hook, line, and sinker.

I realized now that, although I was made in the image of God, I was not God or a part of God in any way. God was God, and I was me. I wasn't Christ or a part of Christ, and neither was Buddha or anyone else. Jesus was the Christ, and there was no other. And, in spite of what anyone else tried to say, He *had* won an amazing victory on the cross of Calvary—one that Joy and I had learned to call on time after time. It was a victory that was fully described in the Scriptures and that so many of the old hymns proclaimed.

Something very mysterious had happened on that "old rugged cross" that a whole New Age was doing hand-over-head flips to completely avoid. It was the "victory in Jesus" that *A Course in Miracles* was desperately trying to redefine and explain away. It was the "amazing grace" that had saved the likes of Joy and me.

Finally, after all we had been through, I was starting to see that the heart of the gospel is not so much that God helps those who help themselves but, rather, that God helps those who *can't* help themselves. It was not in affirming our strength but in recognizing our weakness that we had finally learned to ask the Lord for help. It was His grace, not our own self-sufficiency that had saved the day.

Yet even though we had recognized our need to be saved from the evil that was coming at us, we had stubbornly refused to acknowledge Jesus as our personal Lord and Saviour. Clinging tenaciously to our metaphysical identities, we hadn't understood that our faith ultimately had to be in Jesus, not in ourselves, and that Jesus meant it when He said:

> I am the way, the truth, and the life: no man cometh unto the Father, but by me. (John 14:6)

We had put our faith in ourselves as God and not in God as God; by going within we had gone without. We had grossly underestimated our ability to not be deceived, and we had grossly overestimated the wisdom of our metaphysical teachers.

But thank God for Johanna Michaelsen and her book in the bookstore. It had taken us a while to put everything together, but we were finally starting to see the bigger picture.

I put my notes and papers away and went to tell Joy she had been right once again. After telling her all that I had learned, we talked late into the night about the deception, false teachings, false gospel, and most especially the false Christ of *A Course in Miracles* and the New Age.

Extremely sobered by how different the world looked through the microscopic lens of the Bible instead of the rose-colored glasses of the Course and the New Age, Joy and I were thankful for all that we were being shown.

But even in a week of many surprises, our biggest surprise was yet to come. It was not until the next morning that it finally hit me, and when it did it was like spiritual checkmate as all of our past idealism met our present reality and our past cynicism and judgmental attitudes collided with our new beliefs.

4

J oy, I can't believe it—we're *Christians!*"

I looked at Joy in astonishment and with a great sense of irony and even dismay as I suddenly understood that we had just walked into our own least likely scenario.

My words seemed to hang in the air, as we weren't about to deny our new faith, but we weren't about to celebrate it either. We both felt immediately mocked by our past definitions of the word *Christian*. Images of "I found it" buttons, sugary sweet church people, and insincere, money-hungry televangelists flashed through our minds.

It was almost too much to comprehend. Flying high on our spiritual journey, we had been shot down by the truth and now found ourselves parachuting right into the middle of the Christian church. For two people who had been deeply committed to alternative spirituality, it was the ultimate cosmic joke. We had been cornered by our own convictions. But we were now already squirming in this suit of clothes that we never thought we'd ever wear.

Thrilled with our new understanding about the real Christ, we were anything but thrilled with the idea of being lumped together with all those who called themselves Christians. Would we suddenly be able to relate to a group of people to whom we'd never been able to relate before?

Regarding day-to-day Christians as unbelievable, we had assumed their Bible was, too. But in judging the Bible by those who claimed to follow it, we had made the infamous mistake of judging the book by its cover. And in fleeing from the superficiality and hypocrisy that we thought we saw in Christians, we had run directly into the welcoming arms of our metaphysical teachers. We had been only too glad to have those teachers redefine Christ, His teachings, and anything that had to do with traditional Christianity.

We had been so thoroughly turned off by Christians that we had been ready for almost anything else that would put the spirit back into spirituality. The only trouble was that we were so ignorant of the Bible's teachings that we knew nothing of its warnings about spiritual deception or that those who were sincerely deceived, as we had been, would also become a part of that deception.

So although Joy and I were wholeheartedly willing to surrender our lives to the real Christ, we were still reluctant to surrender ourselves to the label of being "Christian." It was hard to get used to the idea that we would now be identified with a group of people we had always regarded with suspicion and disdain. Now we would be on the receiving end of the same condescending smiles and patronizing comments that we used to dish out.

Even so, we knew what we had been through and what we had learned. As we thought about what lay before us, we knew that being Christians would mean a great deal more than going to church on Sunday. With a strong adversary and spiritual deception everywhere, trying to follow the real Christ in this world was going to be an incredible challenge. But as we thought about it, we accepted that if being Christian meant following the true Christ with all of our heart and soul and mind, then we would actually be very pleased to be known as Christians.

Fifteen

The Gospel Truth

When we could finally see through the spiritual deception, most of the Scriptures we had been reading clicked into place. It was as if scales had fallen from our eyes, and suddenly the New Testament was flooded with light. Though we had a lot to learn about other aspects of the faith, it was apparent that we were, by virtue of our having been so thoroughly deceived, already well-versed in the Bible's description of deception.

Several weeks later, after much study, reflection, prayer, and many more talks with Joy, I sat down by the creek one morning, determined to go through the Scriptures and Johanna's book, laying out in even more detail what they said about *A Course in Miracles* and the other false teachings that had been woven into our lives. I went back and forth through the Scriptures trying to piece together our spiritual story.

One of the first passages I looked at talked about "another gospel" and how susceptible we can be to false teachings that try to change the gospel of Christ:

> I marvel that ye are so soon removed from him that called you into the grace of Christ unto another gospel: Which is not another; but there be some that trouble you, and would pervert the gospel of Christ. (Galatians 1:6-7)

I also reread the Scripture quoted in Johanna's book that talked about "another Jesus"—how even those who have already accepted the true Jesus and His Holy Spirit could be deceived by a false Christ.

For if he that cometh preacheth another Jesus, whom
we have not preached, or *if* ye receive another spirit,
which ye have not received, or another gospel, which
ye have not accepted, ye might well bear with *him*.
(2 Corinthians 11:4)

Helen Schucman heard an "inner voice" that said, "This is *A
Course in Miracles*. Please take notes." The voice, which later identified itself as "Jesus," proceeded to dictate a body of material that
completely contradicted the real gospel of Christ and whose oppositional teachings could only be characterized as "another gospel,"
"another spirit," and "another Jesus." Most of us who had read, studied, and believed in *A Course in Miracles* never knew or took seriously the Bible's explicit warnings about the deceivers who would come
in Christ's name and pretend to be Him.

And most of us never knew the Bible's explicit warnings that
false Christs and false prophets would arise in our midst and se-
duce us with supernatural signs and wonders to make us think their
teachings came from God. Those signs and wonders would be so
convincing that "if it were possible" they would fool even the most
faithful believers of the real gospel and the real Christ.

For there shall arise false Christs, and false prophets,
and shall show great signs and wonders; insomuch
that, if *it were* possible, they shall deceive the very elect.
(Matthew 24:24)

But even if we had been aware of the warnings, who would
have ever suspected that these false Christs and prophets would arise
within our very selves and within our spiritual friends and teachers?
Certainly the "Jesus" that arose within Helen Schucman and mani-
fested as an audible "inner voice" was proof to us all that false Christs
and false prophets were not always flesh and blood but could also
come in the form of lying spirits pretending to be a "spirit guide,"

the "Holy Spirit," our "higher self," or, in Helen's case, "Jesus." The lying spirits delivered not only false counsel but also false teachings, such as *A Course in Miracles.*

> Now the Spirit speaketh expressly, that in the latter times some shall depart from the faith, giving heed to seducing spirits, and doctrines of devils. (1 Timothy 4:1)

Just so there would be no mistake about where the lying spirits came from and how they operated, the Bible spelled it out in even more detail. I looked at the Scripture Johanna quoted on the last page of her book.

> For such are false apostles, deceitful workers, transforming themselves into the apostles of Christ. And no marvel; for Satan himself is transformed into an angel of light. Therefore, *it is* no great thing if his ministers also be transformed as the ministers of righteousness; whose end shall be according to their works. (2 Corinthians 11:13-15)

An angel of darkness could cleverly disguise himself as an angel of light. His servants could disguise themselves as teachers of Christ or even as Christ Himself. They were deceivers of darkness from the other side—another gospel, another spirit, another Christ—the ultimate deception. We certainly hadn't gone out looking for deception, but in our spiritual ignorance we had walked right into their clever trap.

The Scriptures had been prophetic as they described in detail the signs and wonders and false prophets and false Christs and lying spirits. Many of us had been so convinced we were on the right path that we never stopped to question the source of "the Source" or any of the other voices that seemed to be divinely inspired, and just as Helen Schucman's "inner voice" went unchallenged, so did our own inner voices and those of our spiritual teachers.

In fact, the Bible had not only predicted spiritual deception but actually warned us to test the spirits before we listened to them:

> Beloved, believe not every spirit, but try the spirits whether they are of God: because many false prophets are gone out into the world. Hereby know ye the Spirit of God: Every spirit that confesseth that Jesus Christ is come in the flesh is of God: And every spirit that confesseth not that Jesus Christ is come in the flesh is not of God. (1 John 4:1 -3)

The test is a godly "Halt, who goes there?" to make sure the spirits are really from God. Deceptive spirits cannot say that Jesus is *the* Christ. When strongly challenged, a deceptive spirit will deny that Jesus is the Christ and that He came in the flesh to earth.

In some mysterious, God-appointed way, deceptive spirits cannot withstand the Bible's test any more than they could remain in our presence when we commanded them to leave in the name of Jesus Christ. God mercifully provided us with this way of discerning what is really happening. In fact, the Course's Jesus himself answered the question of whether or not he was the Christ. His answer, "Oh yes, along with you,"[5] clearly failed the Bible's test.

Those of us who had believed the Course's Jesus—that he was the Christ and we were, too—were deceived into thinking that "the Christ" was something bigger than Jesus or us or anyone else. But in believing the Course and my other spiritual teachers, I had unwittingly become the very person the real Jesus warned me to watch out for:

> Take heed that no man deceive you. For many shall come
> in my name, saying, I am Christ; and shall deceive many.
> (Matthew 24:4-5)

From that first psychic reading, I had been deceived. Led down a yellow brick road by pied piper spirits, I had, with the best intentions, landed in a metaphysical New Age where the Christ proclaimed was not the real Christ at all. A well-orchestrated and exquisitely timed series of supernatural synchronistic experiences had convinced me that my involvement in alternative spirituality was "meant to be."

Following the signs and wonders of deceptive spirits, I had jumped through my spiritual hoops with almost flawless precision. With expert strings being pulled by the other side, I had been seduced by a ball of light, an Indian guru on a Big Sur mountaintop, a former Napa Valley farmer who was now channeling "the Source," and *A Course in Miracles* that had been sent by "Jesus." As Joy and I both had unknowingly plugged into the spirit world, we never realized that most of the voices we were listening to were part of the deception the real Jesus had warned about.

In contemplating my former disbelief in the Scriptures, I made one last footnote to my morning study. I thought about the magician I had read about in the Book of Acts—an evil man who used his powers to turn men from God. Paul had seen through the magician's schemes and had directly confronted him, even calling him a child of the devil:

> O full of all subtlety and all mischief, *thou* child of the devil, *thou* enemy of all righteousness, wilt thou not cease to pervert the right ways of the Lord? (Acts 13:10)

How amazing! I thought. *It was the mad magician's first-century cousin.* Just as Paul had seen through the guise of that magician, Joy had seen through the guise of the mad magician.

Magicians. Evil spirits. False teachings from a deceptive spirit world. Even a devil. Pretty common stuff in the first-century, but in our modern, progressive, high-tech world, who would ever believe it was still going on today? Yet after what Joy and I had been through, we had no choice but to believe it. As far removed from reality as those things in the Bible seemed to be, we had just watched it all play out right before our eyes.

What we had thought to be spiritual truth had turned out to be nothing more than fiction. What we had believed to be the fiction of the Bible had ironically turned out to be the gospel truth. The age of deception that had been predicted was already well on its way.

In listening to our spiritual teachers, we had missed the many warnings that were being shouted to us from the pages of the Bible. We were, in reality, fallen human beings, prone to temptation, and easily overcome by evil. And although there was no way we could ever save ourselves, we could be saved by Jesus Christ—the true Son of God—whom God sent to set us free.

I knew now that if being "a sinner" meant falling short and being in need of salvation and redemption, then I was a sinner. And if "repenting" meant turning away from my sins and my ungodly ways, then I was ready to repent. And if being "born again" meant being born again from God on high, then I wanted to be born again.

I knew I had a lot to learn about Jesus and all of His teachings and that being a disciple of His would be the test of my life. But I was grateful that Joy and I had been given a window into the spirit world in what had turned out to be our crash course on the truth of the Bible.

In some strange and wonderful way, Joy and I had backed into the gospel and into our faith. It was only after our whole world had been turned upside down and inside out that we found ourselves right side up at the foot of the cross.

As I gathered my things together and headed up to the house to find Joy, I could hardly believe what was happening. But it was all right there in the Scriptures—the Scriptures that had proven themselves in the heat of our lives.

I thought of where I was now in relation to my faith, and I knew it was time for me to more formally acknowledge my commitment to Christ. I wasn't sure how I would do it, but I knew the inspiration would come from God, not from me, and I would know when the time was right.

Sixteen

Amazing Grace

Aweek or so later, in conjunction with my new job as a consultant for a nonprofit agency serving people with special needs, I met with the youth pastor of a local church. I had been making the rounds of community clubs and organizations, telling them about one of our new programs. But in the middle of my presentation my voice broke, and my thoughts shifted from the subject at hand. Before I knew it, I was telling him all about our spiritual journey.

In great detail, I described what had happened to us in the last six months, including our confrontations with evil and our learning to call on Jesus. As I finished my rather freewheeling account, I told him the bottom line was that I was finally ready to ask the real Jesus into my life to be my Lord and Saviour.

A bit stunned by my departure from the scheduled agenda, the pastor was clearly thrown by my spontaneous midmorning testimony. Certainly it was unusual for a community social worker to interrupt his presentation to say, "I need Jesus!"

Rattled, but wanting to respond to my obvious expression of faith, he reached for his Bible and diligently tracked down what seemed to be all the right Scriptures for such an occasion. I listened respectfully as he read first one and then another.

> For God so loved the world, that he gave his only begotten Son, that whosoever believeth in him should not perish, but have everlasting life. (John 3:16)

> For all have sinned, and come short of the glory of God. (Romans 3:23)

> But God commendeth his love toward us, in that, while
> we were yet sinners, Christ died for us. (Romans 5:8)

> That if thou shalt confess with thy mouth the Lord Jesus,
> and shalt believe in thine heart that God hath raised him
> from the dead, thou shalt be saved. (Romans 10:9)

He also read a Scripture I had noticed several times recently
and that seemed to capture the essence of our new faith:

> For by grace are ye saved through faith; and that not of
> yourselves: it *is* the gift of God: not of works, lest any
> man should boast. (Ephesians 2:8-9)

Finally, the youth pastor looked up and into my eyes. It was
in that moment that we seemed to see in each other all the frailties
and shortcomings of being human. We both knew and understood
how much we needed the Lord's help in our lives and how much we
needed Him to be our Saviour.

We then bowed our heads in prayer, and it was with great emotion and conviction that I prayed:

> Dear Lord, Please forgive me for following spiritual teach-
> ings that have nothing to do with You and for not believ-
> ing Your Scriptures or understanding who You really are.
> I confess my sins and ask that You send Jesus—who died
> for my sins—into my life to be my Lord and Saviour and
> that You send Your Holy Spirit to me. Please continue to
> show me Your truth, and may Your will always be done
> in my life. In Jesus' name, Amen.

When I finished my prayer, there was no earthquake, no thun-
derbolt—just a sense that I had finally done what I needed to do. I
had publicly confessed my faith and converted my intellectual understanding to spiritual reality. Knowing that it was Jesus Himself

who said we should not be surprised that we *must* be born again, it suddenly felt quite right to be "born again."

2

Ten days later, Joy and I were married in a small church wedding in a nearby town. Almost immediately, we felt blessed by the act of marriage as we committed ourselves to each other and to God in what really seemed to be holy matrimony. As we headed out into life together, we could feel a deep peace and conviction moving into our lives.

And with those deep feelings came the natural desire to share what we had learned with our friends—that all of our seeking and yearning was now finally being fulfilled in our new relationship with the real Christ.

Yet as we tried to tell others what we had discovered, we could see that, in general, most of our friends were more embarrassed for us than they were interested in what we had to say. To them our conversion was a stunning betrayal of everything we had stood for over the years. For us to abandon our metaphysical beliefs for something as "outdated" and "narrow-minded" as the literal gospel made no sense to them at all.

So it was with deep sadness that we watched most of our friends suddenly stop talking about anything spiritual in our presence. They seemed to be saying, "Just because you blew it, don't think you are going to lay your trip on me!" As far as others were concerned, we had not found grace but had fallen from it.

However, when we tried to relate to the traditional Christian community, they didn't seem to understand us either. When they asked at churches how we became Christians, and we told them about the black magician, the deceptive spirits, and the spiritual warfare, we were usually directed to the coffee and doughnuts.

Sometimes we thought we were confusing everyone but ourselves. Disappointed but not disheartened by our friends, and discouraged but not disillusioned by some of the churches, we were nevertheless determined to tell our story of the reality of evil and of the power and majesty of the real Christ—how it was the Bible, not our alternative spiritual teachings, that read clearer and truer than the morning paper.

The Bible may seem archaic to a lot of people, but in our trial by fire we had found it to be true. To call on the Lord is a most mysterious and wonderful thing. And we who had been so sure of our metaphysical beliefs were perhaps the most surprised of all to discover the magnitude and depth of our new convictions.

Standing on the threshold of a whole new spiritual adventure, Joy and I marveled at our situation. Like Jonah of old, we had fled as far as we could from the God of the Bible. But in our confrontation with darkness, we had found that the God of the Bible was not in the box we thought we had Him in. In fact, He had been patiently and lovingly waiting for us to see the light and come around.

We had come to realize that one is either for the Lord or against Him—there is no middle ground. It had to be the Christ of the Bible or the Christ of the New Age.

In dismay, we watched unsuspecting Christians study A Course in Miracles in their churches and even invite metaphysical/New Age speakers to teach from their pulpits. Clearly, many who said they were of "the faith" would soon become a part of the deception, too, if they weren't already.

Were we witnessing the great "falling away" predicted in the Bible (2 Thessalonians 2:3)? Was the "mystery of iniquity" talk-ed about in the Scriptures already doing its deceptive work with "all power and signs and lying wonders" and "all deceivableness of unrighteousness" (2 Thessalonians 2:7-10)? Would people calling themselves Christians abandon their faith in the Bible and the Bible's Christ (1 Timothy 4:1)? Would they join an ecumenical movement that in the name of love, God, unity, and peace would sacrifice the truth of the Bible and perhaps one day merge with the New Age itself? Jesus warned that such a faith would lead not to life but to ultimate destruction:

> Enter ye in at the strait gate: for wide *is* the gate, and broad *is* the way, that leadeth to destruction, and many there be which go in thereat: Because strait *is* the gate, and narrow *is* the way, which leadeth unto life, and few there be that find it. (Matthew 7:13-14)

But thanks to a massage client, a mad magician, and the saving grace of the real Christ, Joy and I had seen the light and found the narrow way. Although we knew that we would be misunderstood, disbelieved, ridiculed, and even hated, we knew what we had seen and experienced and come to believe. And we knew we could now state with other believers that we had been eyewitnesses to the majesty and power of the Lord Jesus Christ.

> For we have not followed cunningly devised fables, when we made known unto you the power and coming of our Lord Jesus Christ, but were eyewitnesses of his majesty. (2 Peter 1:16)

May the Lord bless you and open your eyes to any deception that may be in your life. And may you always remember in your heart of hearts to pray for the truth.

Epilogue

Since the original 1992 publication of *The Light That Was Dark,* the New Age movement has expanded its reach into almost every aspect of society—including the evangelical Church. Unfortunately, most Christian leaders have not been watchful, and as a result the Church is in the process of being greatly deceived. In my 2004 book, *Deceived on Purpose,* I wrote:

> But even with all of these open threats and challenges to biblical Christianity, most Christian leaders today continue to generally ignore almost anything having to do with New Age teachers and teachings. Over the last decade, as New Age teachings exploded in popularity, church leaders suddenly became very quiet about the New Age. Perhaps distracted by church growth concerns and tracking what they considered to be the latest "moves of God," church leaders seemed to be missing the latest moves of our spiritual Adversary. Excited about all of the "great" things they felt God was doing, they had become ignorant of what our Adversary was doing.[6]

This heightened lack of discernment in the Church was brought home to me in a very personal way. The New Age leader who introduced me to the deceptive teachings of *A Course in Miracles* was a special guest on the television ministry of one of America's "most trusted" mainline pastors.[7] It was an amazing sign of the times to listen to this avowed Christian minister and this veteran New Age leader exchange spiritual pleasantries as they mutually endorsed each other's books in front of millions of viewers.[8] Equally amazing was the fact that earlier in the year this same pastor had been one of the featured speakers at the annual conference for the National Association of Evangelicals.[9]

Unfortunately, in its attempt to reach the world, today's Church is becoming more and more like the world. There is little difference today between the holy and the profane. Mysticism and spiritual experience are taking precedence over biblical discernment and truth. The mystery of iniquity is masquerading as the mystery of godliness, while the Church is being methodically transitioned into the New Age. A personal saving relationship with the true Jesus Christ is giving way to "another Jesus," "another gospel," and "another spirit." Sadly, hardly anyone seems to notice or care.

Today, our spiritual Adversary is purposefully tempting everyone in the world and in the Church to *change* with the times and to accept his fresh new approach to spirituality and divinity. Using a wide range of deceived spiritual leaders, he is reaching out to humanity with a peace plan that is based on universal New Age principles. He is promising world peace to those who are willing to enlarge their beliefs enough to accept the bottom-line teaching of his New Spirituality—that we are all one because God is in everyone and everything.

The professing Christian Church does not seem to understand how it is walking right into this most ingeniously contrived spiritual trap. Placing its faith in men and mass movements rather than in properly translated and rightly divided Scripture, the Church is starting to adopt some of the *very same teachings* I renounced when I left the New Age. Please don't fall for these false teachings.

When the New Age teachings of the New Spirituality present themselves as a "fresh" new approach to traditional biblical Christianity, stand fast against them. Don't be enticed by them. Be watchful. Be vigilant. Be steadfast in the faith. Know that our spiritual Adversary is seducing the Church today with many of the same devices that he used to draw me into the New Age so many years ago.

Not everything that happens in your life is from God. There *is* a Deceiver. Prove all things. Hold on to that which is good. Love the truth. Put your faith in God's Word, not in man's word.

The Lord Jesus Christ warned that great deception in the world and in the Church would precede His return. Those days are definitely here. Beware of the mystical, New Age teachings that are starting to characterize today's emerging Church. Beware of die New Spirituality that is knocking at your door.

Beware of the light that is dark.

Endnotes

1. Foundation for Inner Peace, *A Course in Miracles: Combined Volume (Text, Workbook for* Students, *Manual for Teachers)* (Glen Ellen, CA: Foundation for Inner Peace, 1975, 1992), *(Workbook for Students),* pp. 53, 119, 166, 222, 284.

2. Ibid., p. 216.

3. Ibid., pp. 77, 284, 51.

4. Johanna Michaelsen, *The Beautiful Side of Evil* (Eugene, OR: Harvest House, 1982), pp. 147-148.

5. Foundation for Inner Peace, *A Course in Miracles: Combined Volume (Manual for Teachers),* p. 87.

6. Warren Smith, *Deceived on Purpose: The New Age Implications of the Purpose-Driven Church* (Magalia, CA: Mountain Stream Press, 2004), p. 17.

7. http://www.barna.org/HexPage.aspxJPage=BarnaUpdate Narro&wekBarnaUpdateID =178 (link no longer accessible).

8. https://web.archive.org/web/20080211190826/http://www.hou-rofpower.org/interviews/interviews_detail.cfm?ArticleID=3079.

9. National Association of Evangelicals: Annual conference, March 11, 2004, Robert Schuller, NAE Compact Disc.

Also by Warren B. Smith

The Titanic and Today's Church
A Tale of Two Shipwrecks

The Titanic and Today's Church is the story of two shipwrecks. One took place over a century ago; the other is in progress and is happening today. The similarities are astounding as they compel us to become more aware of our Spiritual Adversary's schemes and devices (2 Corinthians 2:11), effectively "stand against" them (Ephesians 6:11), and "come out from among them" (2 Corinthians 6:17). 264 pages, $14.95. Softbound.

The Light That Was Dark:
From the New Age to Amazing Grace

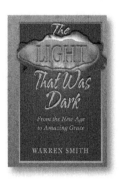

The personal account of how Warren B. Smith, who as a spiritual seeker, was led into the metaphysical New Age where the Christ proclaimed wasn't the real Christ at all. Concerned that today's church is being seduced by the same false teachings and the same false Christ that drew him into the New Age, Smith shares his story in a most compelling way. 168 pages, 2nd edition. $14.95. Softbound.

A "Wonderful" Deception:
The Further New Age Implications of the Emerging Purpose Driven Movement

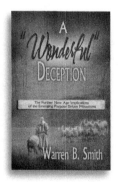

Five years after writing *Deceived On Purpose* Warren Smith continues to reveal how Christian leaders wittingly or unwittingly are leading the church into a spiritual trap. *A "Wonderful" Deception* examines church metaphors, concepts, and beliefs that are essentially the same as those being used in today's New Age/New Spirituality teachings. 242 Pages. $14.95. Softbound.

Warren Smith's books are published by Mountain Stream Press. For wholesale and retail orders contact 866-876-3910. For other book, DVD, and booklet titles by Warren Smith, visit www.newagetoamazinggrace.com.

Made in the USA
Middletown, DE
16 March 2022

62721208R10096